ESSENTIALS
OF ENGLISH

RAPID-REFERENCE KEY

The following is an English essentials key, arranged according to problem area, of the topics discussed in this book. The number indicated at the right of each item refers to the section of the book in which that topic is discussed.

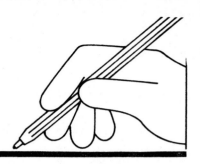

Logic and Clarity

Misused Words and Expressions

ESSENTIALS OF ENGLISH

Third Edition

Vincent F. Hopper
Cedric Gale
Formerly of New York University

Ronald C. Foote
California State University, Long Beach

Revised by
Benjamin W. Griffith
West Georgia College

BARRON'S EDUCATIONAL SERIES, INC.
Woodbury, New York • London • Toronto • Sydney

All inquiries should be addressed to:
Barron's Educational Series, Inc.
113 Crossways Park Drive
Woodbury, New York 11797

Library of Congress Catalog Card No. 81-10797
International Standard Book No. 0-8120-2283-1

Library of Congress Cataloging in Publication Data
Hopper, Vincent Foster, 1906-
    Essentials of English.
    Includes index.
    1. English language—Grammar—1950-   2. English
language—Rhetoric. I. Gale, Cedric, 1905-
II. Foote, Ronald C. III. Griffith, Benjamin W.
IV. Title.
PE1112.H64 1981   428.2   81-10797
ISBN 0-8120-2283-1   AACR2

PRINTED IN THE UNITED STATES OF AMERICA

6789   510   16 15 14 13 12 11 10

CONTENTS

The Sentence and Its Parts

Sentence Errors

Logic and Clarity

Emphasis, Consistency, and Appropriateness

Punctuation

The Paragraph

The Writer's Approach to the Subject

PREFACE

Though good advice on good writing stands the test of time and needs little revision, *Essentials of English* is also a practical grammar which has needed revision because all grammars need revising. The study of grammar has taken a quantum step in the last ten years so that, to a degree, all grammars have suffered some obsolescence. Therefore, it has been necessary to revise the grammar sections of this handbook in order to exploit new interest in and insight into syntax and to reaffirm the close connection between the good analysis of structure and the writing of good prose.

This edition, like its predecessors, attempts to give the potential writer an expert command of the fundamentals of good English usage and the basic skills required for effective writing. In systematic fashion, it proceeds from analysis of English words to sentences. It continues with instruction on matters like logic, clarity, emphasis, consistency, and punctuation. It concludes with advice on handling the larger elements such as the paragraph and the whole composition.

Essentials of English may be studied as a course, proceeding from the simple to the more complex. Students may practice each principle in turn and be assured of their progress by using the companion volume *Practice for Effective Writing*. If they have difficulty in spelling, Mersand's *Spelling Your Way to Success* will complete the study aids that the students will require to become dependable and effective writers.

The authors have also kept in mind the persistent need of writers for a compact, ready reference work. Consequently, the diversified contents are clearly demarked and are readily identifiable to facilitate the finding of specific principles or answers to particular problems of composition. Instructors in the communication arts may refer students to specified numbered sections for guidance in their areas of weakness.

Essentials of English aims to be comprehensive without being cumbersome. It seeks, in all areas, to be exact, clear, succinct.

NOTE: Throughout this edition, an asterisk will be used to indicate an ungrammatical form in Standard American English.

The Word

Just as expert carpenters must be thoroughly acquainted with the tools of their craft and as artists must have expert knowledge of colors, so good writers must have a thorough understanding of the basic material with which they work: **words.** Thoughts and utterances, both simple and complex, require words of several kinds—for example, naming words, asserting words, connecting words, descriptive words. One of the first steps to effective writing is, therefore, a knowledge of the properties and functions of the different kinds of words. This knowledge involves what a word looks like, where it appears, and what it does within its context.

1 The Noun

The noun is a naming word. It is used to identify people, places, objects, ideas, emotions—in short, anything that can be named: *John, Harlem, committee, amplification, table, hatred, baseball.*

1A Recognition of Nouns

Nouns can be recognized by their form and their position in the sentence as well as by their naming function. Below are some of the things to look for when you are trying to identify the nouns in a sentence. (The things listed here are discussed in greater detail in other sections of the book.)

(1) Most nouns can follow the word *the* or other determiners such as *my, a, this: a truth, his moves, this infiltration.*

(2) All nouns can occur before and after verbs: *His* **moves** *dazzled the* **spectators. Faith** *moves* **mountains.**

(3) All nouns can follow relationship words called prepositions: *before winter, after Christmas, in his adversity.*

(4) Most nouns can take an *s* or an *es* at the end of the word to express the idea of more than one: *soup, soups; church, churches; debate, debates.*

(5) Some nouns can take an apostrophe and an *s* or an apostrophe by itself to express belonging: *the* **boy's** *bicycle; the* **boys'** *room;* **Dickens'** *novels.*

(6) Some nouns can start with a capital letter to indicate the name or the title of some specific thing or person: *Wilson High School, Armando, America, September, Jew, Surgeon General.*

(7) Some nouns have endings such as *-ness, -tion, -ity,* whose function is to indicate that the word is a noun: *reasonableness, adversity, infiltration.*

1B Proper and Common Nouns

The name or title of an individual, of a person, place, or thing is usually expressed by a proper noun or nouns. They are always capitalized. When these nouns do *not* refer to the name of a person or thing, they are common nouns and are *not* capitalized. Compare:

> I will ask *Mother.*
> Yesterday she became a *mother.*

> I think that *Crescent City* is in Alberta.
> The *city* lay on a crescent in the river.

He settled in the *West.*
He drove *west* for ten miles.

Among other things, proper nouns name people, continents, countries, provinces, states, counties, parishes, geographic regions, days of the week, months of the year, holidays, festivals (but not seasons): *Christmas, winter, December, Friday, Alberta, the Netherlands, Judge, Hernandez.*

1C Singular and Plural Nouns

Most nouns can be singular or plural in form. The usual plural form adds *s* or *es* to the end of the word: *sigh, sighs; fox, foxes; category, categories; calf, calves.* Note that the *y* and the *f* change before a plural ending. **Trys* and **Skys* are incorrect forms. There is less consistency with the *f* forms. *Hoofs* is possible; **rooves* is not. It is advisable to have a dictionary at hand when dealing with some plurals.

Some nouns have irregular plural forms: *child, children; goose, geese; sheep, sheep.* Some nouns borrowed from other languages keep their original plural forms: *datum, data; cherub, cherubim; crisis, crises; formula, formulae.* Note that *formula* is used so frequently that the incorrect form **formulas* is being used by some educated speakers. It is sometimes advisable to have an up-to-date dictionary on hand when you are faced with foreign plurals.

Some nouns can normally occur in the singular form only: *much dust, *much dusts; more courage, *more courages; less fun, *less funs.* These nouns are called mass nouns or non-countable nouns. Note that some determiners such as *much* and *less* work only with non-countable nouns although recently there has been a tendency among educated speakers to use **less people* (*people* is a countable noun) rather than *fewer people.*

A few non-countable nouns can appear in the plural form if the idea of a difference of kind is stressed. *There are some new instant coffees on the market. Several wheats grow in Australia.*

*Throughout the text, an asterisk will be used to indicate an ungrammatical form in Standard American English.

1D   The Possessive Case of Nouns

The possessive case of nouns is formed by adding an apostrophe and an *s* to words which do not end with an *s* or a *z* sound: *the boy's room, the children's school;* and by adding only the apostrophe to words which do end with an *s* or a *z* sound: *the boys' room, Dickens' novel.* If, however, the word ending in *s* or *z* is a proper noun with only one syllable, an apostrophe and an *s* are added to the word: *Keats's sonnets, Santa Claus's reindeer.*

NOTE: Some classical names and other names that would be awkward to pronounce with an added apostrophe and *s* use only the apostrophe: *Xerxes' chariot, Moses' tablets.*

Care must be taken in forming the possessive form of nouns ending with *y* because although the singular and plural forms sound the same way, they are spelled differently.

> the baby's cry [one baby's cry]
>
> the babies' murmurings [the murmurings of several babies]

When possession is shared by two or more nouns, this fact is indicated by using the possessive case for the last noun in the series: *Jose, Fred, and Edward's canoe.*

When two nouns refer to the same person, the second noun is in the possessive case.

> *the mother of the bride's yellow dress* [The bride probably wore white. If the phrase sounds awkward, the use of two possessives does not improve it much: *the bride's mother's yellow dress.*] Better: *The yellow dress of the bride's mother.*

1E   The Apostrophe Possessive and the "OF" Possessive

Non-animate things do not normally "possess" anything. The possessive form using the preposition *of* is used in order to express an arrangement or part of non-animate things.

piles of coats **NOT** *coats' piles
the edge of the chisel **NOT** *the chisel's edge

However, writers have long made exception to this rule in such matters as time, money, and transportation: *a day's work, a dollar's worth, the ship's compass.* Today more and more non-animate things are taking the apostrophe form of the possessive: *the razor's edge, the book's success, education's failure.* Obviously, no clear rule can be stated where *the razor's edge* is approved of and **the chisel's edge* is frowned on.

1F Functions of Nouns

The noun can perform a variety of functions. The functions listed here are discussed in greater detail in other sections of the book.

(1) *The noun can work as the subject, object, or complement of a finite verb or verbal.*

> Being a recent *arrival* [complement of the verbal *being*] from Puerto Rico, *Margarita* [subject of the verb *was*] was proud that she could speak *Spanish* [object of the verb *speak*] as well as English.

(2) *The noun can work as the object of a preposition.*

> Margarita, who came from *Puerto Rico* [object of the preposition *from*], spoke excellent Spanish in her *home* [object of the preposition *in*] and good English at *school* [object of the preposition *at*].

(3) *The noun can work after another noun as a modifier or an appositive, as it is also called.*

> my brother *Charles*
> his problem, a damaged *retina*

(4) *The noun can work before another noun as a modifier.*

> a *problem* child   a *noun* clause   a *bottle* opener

(5) *The noun can work as a modifier of an adjective or a verb.*

They were *battle* weary. [modifier of the adjective *weary*]

They arrived *yesterday.* [modifier of the verb *arrived*]

(6) *The noun in the possessive case can work as a determiner introducing another noun.*

the *bride's mother* [*The bride's* introduces *mother.* The article *the* belongs to *bride's,* not to *mother.*]

---

2 The Pronoun

Although a pronoun often takes the place of a noun in a sentence, the pronoun is sometimes a word which lacks specific meaning. Indefinite pronouns like *anyone, something, somebody* mean only that unspecified people or things are being referred to.

When pronouns replace other words, they carry the meaning of these replaced words. The replaced words are called the **antecedent** of the pronoun. The antecedent of a pronoun is usually a noun and its modifiers, if any, but sometimes the antecedent can be a whole sentence.

The dog lost *its* bone. [*Its* replaces *the dog.*]

The old man, *who* had his car stolen, was in shock. [*Who* replaces *the old man.*]

I have written to my younger sister, who lives in Las Piedras, to invite *her* to the wedding. [*Her* replaces *my younger sister, who lives in Las Piedras.*]

Do you want a small cone or a large *one?* [*One* replaces *cone.* It is a special pronoun which allows us to replace the noun and retain its modifiers.]

Lumsden tried to calm his wife's fears. He found *this* harder than he expected. [*This* replaces the whole sentence dealing with an attempt to calm fears.]

2A Personal Pronouns

The personal pronouns are distinguished by person, case, and number.

FIRST PERSON (the person speaking or writing)

Case	Singular	Plural
Nominative	I	we
Possessive	my, mine	our, ours
Objective	me	us

SECOND PERSON (the person addressed)

Case	Singular	Plural
Nominative	you	you
Possessive	your, yours	your, yours
Objective	you	you

In the third person, pronouns are also distinguished by gender.

THIRD PERSON (the person, place, or thing spoken or written about)

Case	Singular			Plural
	MASCULINE	FEMININE	NEUTER	
Nominative	he	she	it	they
Possessive	his	her, hers	its	their, theirs
Objective	him	her	it	them

2B Relative Pronouns

When a sentence is embedded inside another sentence to function as a relative clause, a relative pronoun replaces the repeated noun in order to make the new sentence grammatical.

> *Magic Johnson—Magic Johnson has all the moves—could not be stopped.

> Magic Johnson, *who* has all the moves, could not be stopped.

> *The tools—he bought the tools yesterday—were specked with rust.

The tools *which* he bought yesterday were specked with rust.

Who, whom, whose, that refer to people; *which, of which, that* refer to things. Sometimes the relative pronoun can be omitted altogether: *The tools he bought yesterday were specked with rust.*

2C Interrogative Pronouns

The interrogative pronouns *who, whom, whose, which, what* are some of the words that introduce questions. *Who, whom,* and *whose* indicate that the expected answer will be a person; *what* indicates that the answer will be something nonhuman; *which* may be used for either persons or things.

Who was the chairman?	Answer:	John
What was he carrying?	Answer:	a suitcase
Which girl was hurt?	Answer:	Justine

2D Demonstrative Pronouns

The demonstrative pronouns *this, these, that, those* indicate nearness to or distance from the speaker, literally or figuratively. The antecedent of the pronoun usually is in another clause or sentence. Sometimes the reference is too general for there to be a specific antecedent.

This is my father, Mr. Rodriguez, and *those* are my children, Juanita and Armando. [The antecedent *Mr. Rodriguez* is literally closer to the speaker than are his children.]

Marcellus would climb trees at night. *This* disturbed his mother. [The antecedent of *this* is the sentence about Marcellus' nocturnal tree-climbing.]

Be gentle to *those* who stay angry. [*Those* has no antecedent, in the normal sense of the word. The reference is limited by the following relative clause.]

Demonstrative pronouns frequently work with nouns: *this event, these children.* This function is discussed in the section on determiners. (See Section 9E [4].)

2E Indefinite Pronouns

The indefinite pronouns are so named because their antecedents are usually vague or unknown. These are such words as *each, all, either, anyone, somebody, everyone, whoever, whatever.* They form the possessive case in the same manner as nouns: *anyone's, somebody else's.* (See also Section 2K.)

2F Intensive and Reflexive Pronouns

Personal pronouns ending with *self* or *selves* (*myself, ourselves, itself,* etc.) have two functions. The first is to repeat the noun antecedent in order to emphasize and intensify the meaning: *Mary herself was responsible.* The second function is also to repeat the noun antecedent but in a different part of the sentence.

> *I* hurt *myself.* [*Myself* repeats *I*, but it functions as the object while the antecedent *I* functions as the subject.]

Myself should not be used in place of *me*: *He is going to the hockey game with Michelle and *myself.* [*Me* should be used.]

2G Pronoun Case

Case is a form change which denotes the relation of a noun or a pronoun to other words in the sentence. In English, nouns have only one form change which could be called a case change—the apostrophe form (possessive case). (See Section 1D.) Some pronouns have three or four case forms. They are the personal pronouns and the two relative pronouns *who* and *whoever.*

2H   The Nominative or Subject Case

The pronoun forms *I, we, you, it, he, she, they, who, whoever* are in the nominative case. The uses of the nominative case follow:

(1) *Expressing a subject:*

Jason and *I* are going to the pizza parlor. [*Me and Jason and *Jason and me are not acceptable in the standard dialect.]

I don't know *who* stole the peach tree. [*Who* is the subject of *stole.*]

Give it to *whoever* comes. [*Whoever* is the subject of *comes,* not the object of *to.* The object of *to* is the whole clause *whoever comes.*]

(2) *Expressing the subject repeated:*

Three members of our club gave woodwind recitals— Glynis, Paul, and *I.* [The subject is repeated by *Glynis, Paul, and I.* This repeated structure is called an **appositive.**]

(3) *Expressing the subject when the verb is deleted:*

He is more articulate than *she.* [The verb *is* has been deleted.]

He plays as well as *I.* [The verb *play* has been deleted. Many speakers find this construction unduly self-conscious, so they add a word which takes the place of a verb: He *plays as well as I do.*

(4) *Coming after the verb be:* Some educated speakers find the nominative case after *be* so artificial that they will sometimes prefer to use the accusative form of the pronoun.

It was *they* who found the dog.

That must be *she.* [ACCUSATIVE: That must be *her.*]

It is I. [ACCUSATIVE: It is *me.*]

I shouldn't care to be *he*. [ACCUSATIVE: I shouldn't care to be *him*.]

2I The Accusative or Objective Case

The pronoun forms *me, us, her, him, them, whom, whomever* are in the accusative case. There is no case distinction for *you* and *it* in the accusative. The same is true, in English, for all nouns. The uses of the accusative case follow:

(1) *Expressing the object of a verb, verbal, or preposition:*

Shoving *me* before *him*, he forced *me* down the alley.

My brother came between Carlos and *me*. [Sometimes people will say **between Carlos and I* under the mistaken impression that polite people always say *I* rather than *me*.]

Whom were they talking about? [*Whom* is the object of the preposition *about*. In writing, *whom* must always be used in this context. In speaking, *who* is becoming acceptable: *Who were they talking about?*]

Give it to *whomever* he sends to your office. [*Whomever* is the object of the verb *sends*. Again, in speaking, *whoever* is becoming acceptable in this context.]

(2) *Expressing the object repeated:*

The police ticketed three members of our group, Garcia, McEwan, and *me*.

A lot of *us* kids were hurt in the riot.

(3) *Expressing the object when the verb is deleted:*

Mr. Anderson did not recommend him as highly as *me*. [*As he did me* is also possible here.]

(4) *Expressing the nominal before the infinitive:*

We wanted *him* to suffer. [A nominal is a word that is not a noun but functions as one.]

The plan was for *him* to slide down the rope.

2J The Genitive or Possessive Case

There are two sets of pronoun forms in the genitive case:

(1) my   our   your   her   his   its   their   whose

(2) mine   ours   yours   hers   his   its   theirs   whose

The first set of pronouns function as noun modifiers (*his escape, my wife*) and are called here **possessives.** The second set of pronouns function as nominals. (This is *mine; Whose* were found?) and are called here **independent possessives.**

As we have seen, nouns (Section 1D) and indefinite pronouns (Section 2E) also have a genitive case. For convenience, examples of both nouns and pronouns will be given in this section on pronouns.

2K Functions of Possessives

(1) *Possessives function as determiners before nouns.* (See Section 9E [4].) The meanings usually conveyed by these possessive determiners are possession, connection, the performer of an act, and the classification of a thing.

Whose car was stolen? [The question asks about the possession of a car.]

the *bureau's* lawyers [The bureau does not possess the lawyers so much as the lawyers are connected to the bureau.]

(2) *Possessives function in gerund phrases as the introducer of the phrase.* They also function as the substitute for the

nominative case which expresses the performer of the action. Thus *He was leaving* becomes *his leaving.*

> *His* leaving at dawn upset his father.
>
> He slipped away without *anybody's* noticing him.
>
> The *girl's* singing of Brahms's "Lullaby" was musical. [This gerund phrase must not be confused with a participle phrase, which in the following sentence modifies the nominative case *girl: The girl singing in the next room is my sister.*]

There are some exceptions to the rule that gerund phrases are started by a possessive noun or pronoun.

> He slipped away without *anybody* in the room noticing him. [The possessive form is not used because it does not immediately precede the gerund.]
>
> Luis saw *him* leaving the parking lot. [After verbs like *see, hear,* and *watch,* the objective form of the pronoun or noun is used.]
>
> Throwing the bola is not easy. [The action is so general that the writer has nobody in particular in mind. Therefore, no noun or pronoun introduces the gerund phrase.]

2L Functions of Independent Possessives

Independent possessives are nominals; that is, they function as subjects, objects, or complements as nouns do.

> I wonder *whose* this is. [*Whose* is the complement of the verb *is.* Note that this *whose* differs from the *who's* in *Who's there?*]
>
> *His* was a fascinating personality. [*His* is the subject of the verb *was.*]

He's a friend of *Mother's* and *mine*. [*Mother's* and *mine* are the objects of the preposition *of*.]

---

3   The Verb

The verb is a word or a group of words which usually express action or a state of being. There are two kinds of verbs that must be distinguished:

(1) **The Finite Verb** works with the subject of the sentence to give a sense of completeness, a sense of a statement having been made.

(2) **The Non-Finite Verb** or **Verbal** works as a nominal (something like a noun) or a modifier. It never works with a subject. It does not give a sense of completeness. Compare:

FINITE	NON-FINITE
The documents *had compromised* him.	the *compromising* documents . . .
The authorities *accused* him of fraud.	the authorities, *having accused* him of fraud, . . .

The forms and functions of the finite verb are discussed in this section. Non-finite verbs or verbals are discussed in Section 5.

3A   Recognition of Finite Verbs

Finite verbs can be recognized by their form and their position in the sentence. Here are some of the things to look for when you are trying to identify the finite verbs in a sentence:

(1) Most finite verbs can take an *ed* or a *d* at the end of the word to indicate time in the past: *cough, coughed; celebrate, celebrated*. A hundred or so finite verbs do not have these regular endings. They are listed on pages 221-224.

(2) Nearly all finite verbs take an *s* at the end of the word to indicate the present when the subject of the verb is third person singular: *cough, he coughs; celebrate, she celebrates.* The exceptions are auxiliary verbs like *can* and *must.* Remember that nouns can also end in *s.* Thus *the dog races* can refer to a spectator sport or to a fast-moving third person singular dog.

(3) Finite verbs are often groups of words which include such auxiliary verbs as *can, must, have,* and *be: can be suffering, will have gone, must eat.*

(4) Finite verbs usually follow their subjects: *He* **coughs.** *The documents* **had compromised** *him.* *They* **will have gone.**

(5) Finite verbs surround their subjects when some forms of a question are asked: **Is** *he* **coughing? Did** *they* **celebrate?**

3B   Forms of the Finite Verb

Verbs are distinguished by number (singular and plural) and by person (first, second, third). In general, verbs have a different form only in the third person singular of the present tense.

> I, you, we, they *move.*
>
> BUT   He, she, it *moves*

An exception is the verb *to be,* which is more highly inflected:

> SINGULAR   I *am;* you *are;* he, she, it *is*
>
> PLURAL   We, you, they *are.*

In a handbook such as this, it is impossible to present all of the possible forms of the verb. There are literally hundreds of forms which can be produced from one transitive verb.

Instead, we will present the basic ingredients that make up the finite verb and give examples of the more common forms.

The finite verb can be a one-word verb with an indication of present or past tense: *watch, watched; freeze, froze.*

The finite verb can also be a group of words composed of one or more of the following ingredients:

(1) **Modal Auxiliaries:** *will, would, can, must,* etc.

(2) **Perfect Auxiliary:** a part of the verb **have** plus an **-en** or an **-ed** ending.

(3) **Progressive Auxiliary:** a part of the verb **be** plus an **-ing** ending.

(4) **Passive Auxiliary:** a part of the verb **be** plus an **-en** or an **-ed** ending.

(5) **Main Verb:** *watch, tolerate.*

The modal auxiliary is added to the main verb: *(may watch, must watch).* The perfect, progressive, or passive auxiliaries surround the next form of the finite verb. Some examples of this surrounding process follow:

PERFECT   *a part of* **have** plus **ed** surrounding *watch*

he **has** watched you.

PROGRESSIVE   a part of **be** plus **ing** surrounding *watch*

I **was** watching you.

PERFECT   a part of **have** plus **en** surrounding *be;*
PROGRESSIVE   a part of **be** plus **ing** surrounding *watch*

I **had be en** watching you.

Below is a paradigm or layout of some forms of the finite verb *watch.* If all the modal auxiliaries, the singular and plural forms, and the past and present forms were presented, it would take pages to do so. Instead, the following paradigm is limited to forms of the verb using the modal auxiliary *could* and some past forms not using *could.*

MODAL	PERFECT	PROGRESSIVE	PASSIVE
had	watched		
was		watching	
was			watched
had	been	watching	

MODAL		PERFECT	PROGRESSIVE	PASSIVE
	had	been		watched
could	watch			
could	have	watched		
could	be		watching	
could	be			watched
could	have	been	watching	
could	have	been		watched

Progressive perfect passive forms like *could have been being watched* are seldom used; therefore, they have been omitted from the paradigm.

3C   Mood

A verb may be placed in the indicative, imperative, or subjunctive mood to indicate differences in the intention of the speaker or writer.

The indicative mood is used to make an assertion or ask a question.

> The horse *galloped* down the street.

> Where *are* you *going?*

The imperative mood is used for commands, directions, or requests.

> COMMAND   *Go* to the store and *order* a typewriter.

> DIRECTION   *Turn* right at the next traffic light.

> REQUEST   Please *answer* my letter.

Subjunctive Forms

The present and past tense forms of the verb are sometimes used to express matters which are not present or past in the usual sense. They are matters of urgency, formality, possibility, and unreality. The present and past tense forms of the verb used for the subjunctive are not the expected forms. These unexpected forms are called forms of the **subjunctive mood.** (The expected forms are called forms of the **indicative mood.**)

> I demand that he *see* me immediately. [The expected form would be *he sees. He see* conveys an urgent request, a command.]

> I move that the motion *be* tabled. [*Be tabled* rather than the expected *is tabled* expresses the formality desired.]

> It was important that she *love* me. [The present tense form expresses an urgency in the past. The expected past form *that she loved me* is factual rather than urgent.]

> If she *were* to go, there might be trouble. [*If she were* expresses a possibility in the future. There is no trace of past time in this unexpected past tense form.]

> If he *were* talented, he could make money. [The past tense form here indicates that at present he is not talented. It expresses an unreality, a contrary-to-fact situation.]

There are ways to express subjunctive meanings other than using past and present forms of the verb. Auxiliaries such as *might* and *should* can also be used: *If you had been presentable, I might have taken you to the party.*

3D   Transitive and Intransitive Verbs

Verbs are classified as transitive or intransitive.

A transitive verb (*transit* means to *carry,* as in *rapid transit*) requires an object to complete its meaning. The object of a transitive verb is affected, however slightly, by whatever the verb expresses:

> The hammer *struck* the anvil. [The object, *anvil,* has been hit.]

> Angela *read* the newspaper. [The object, *newspaper,* has been read.]

John *has* a horse. [The object, *horse,* is owned.]

An intransitive verb makes an assertion without requiring any object.

The clock *strikes.*

He *walks* down the street every evening.

The bird *is* on the fence.

A copulative verb, a special kind of intransitive verb, is one which connects the subject to a noun, pronoun, or adjective in the predicate.

Sean *is* the president. [*Is* connects *Sean* to *president. Sean* and *president* are the same person. A noun like *president* used after a copulative verb is called a predicate nominative.] In the next two examples, *bluejay* and *I* are predicate nominatives.

The bird *is* a bluejay.

It *is* I.

The most frequently used copulative verb is *to be.* Other commonly used copulative verbs are *become, seem, smell, look, grow, feel, sound, get, taste, appear.*

Many verbs are both transitive and intransitive. A good dictionary will indicate the differences in meaning. In *The hammer strikes the anvil,* the transitive verb *strike* means *to hit.* In a sentence such as *The clock strikes,* the intransitive verb *strike* means to *sound.* The transitive and intransitive meanings of the same verb may be similar, but they are never identical. The statement *He breathes* means that "he" is alive, but *He breathes the mountain air* refers to an experience which "he" is having.

3E The Passive Voice

Transitive verbs can be switched around from the **active voice** to the **passive voice** by a transformation which changes the form of the verb and moves the object into the subject's position. The old subject, if it stays in the sentence, becomes a prepositional phrase starting with *by*. Thus *Sandy Koufax won the award* is transformed into *The award was won by Sandy Koufax.*

The passive voice is used to emphasize or direct attention to the receiver of the action, in this case *the award*. The passive transform switches our attention from *Sandy Koufax* to what he received: *the award.*

The passive voice is also used to eliminate the necessity of naming the agent of the action when that agent is unknown or unimportant.

> Prison authorities released Alfred Krupp from prison in 1951.
>
> Alfred Krupp *was released* from prison in 1951.
>
> Someone stole our car yesterday.
>
> Our car *was stolen* yesterday.

3F Present and Past Tenses

All main verbs are in either the present tense or the past tense: *watch, watched.* The word *tense* is also used for other forms such as perfect and progressive forms.

(1) *The present tense expresses any time which has some element of the present in it, no matter how small.*

> This apple *tastes* good. [a present situation]
>
> Apples *taste* good. [a general truth]
>
> Shakespeare *writes* in blank verse. [He did so in the past, but this fact is still very relevant today.]
>
> In *Hamlet,* the opening scene *takes* place at night. [A play written in the past has a plot summary alive in the present.]
>
> Rita *goes* to Mexico City tomorrow. [The action will occur in the future, but there is a suggestion that the decision to go may have occurred in the present.]
>
> He *uses* lemon in his tea. [a habitual action, past, present, and future]

(2) *The past tense excludes the present and covers those events that took place at a definite time or habitually in the past.* As with the present tense, the meaning is sometimes reinforced by other words which indicate time.

> I *went* down the street yesterday. [a completed event in the past]
>
> Whenever Rocky *went* down the street, the people cheered. [a habitual action in the past]

3G Modal Auxiliaries

Modal auxiliaries express a large variety of ideas and feelings. A few of the more common uses are listed here.

PERMISSION	You *can* put your shirt on now.
	You *may* come in.
ABILITY	I *can* read braille.
	She *could* open the door.
NECESSITY	He *must* see her today.
	He *had* to go to Nairobi.
CONCLUSION	He *must* have seen her.
GENERAL TRUTH	Cats *will* sleep for hours.

3H Future Time

English has no future tense as does Latin. Instead, English uses modal auxiliaries, present and past tense forms, and adverbials of time to express future time.

> He *is going to* lose his mind.
>
> He *is about to* lose his mind.
>
> I *begin* work *tomorrow*.
>
> It's time you *went* to bed.

3I Shall and Will

To indicate simple futurity, formal usage dictates that *shall* is correct for the first person and *will* and *won't* are correct for the second and third persons.

> I (we) *shall* (*shall not*) go.
>
> You *will* (*won't*) go.
>
> He (she, it, they) *will* (*won't*) go.

In recent years, *will* and *won't* are commonly used for all persons even in relatively formal writing. But the *shall* form has persisted in idiomatic expressions, so that *Shall we dance?* or *Shall we go?* are certainly more commonplace than the awkward sounding *Will we dance, go?*

To indicate a promise or determination, *will* is used in the first person: *I (we) will go.* To express a command or determination, *shall* is used in the second and third persons: *You (he, she, it, they) shall go.*

3J Perfect Tenses

A perfect tense is used to talk about an action which occurs at one time but is seen in relation to another time. *I ran out of gas* is a simple statement about a past event. *I've run out of gas* is a statement about a past event which is connected to the present.

> I *have waited* for you. [The present perfect indicates that the action occurred in the past and was completed in the present.]
>
> Luis *has visited* San Juan several times. [The action occurred frequently in the past so that it has become part of Luis' present experience.]
>
> I *had waited* for you. [The past perfect shifts the action further into the past so that it is completed in relation to a later time.]
>
> Mary *had been* out in the canoe all morning when she

suddenly fell into the lake. [The past perfect indicates that, in the past, one event occurred before the other.]

By sundown he *should have finished the job.* [The conditional perfect suggests that something else occurred at a later time to affect the completion of the job.]

By sundown he *will have finished* the job. [The future perfect indicates that the event will be completed by a definite time in the future.]

3K Progressive Tenses

Progressive tenses draw our attention to the continuity of an action rather than its completion. A verb which in its own meaning already expresses a continuity does not need a progressive form. (*I live in Boston* already says it. *I am living in Boston,* the progressive form, says it twice.) But compare *He worked in his cellar* with the progressive form which stresses the continuity of the action: *He was working in his cellar.* The progressive is often helped out by adverbials which express continuity.

He *is always running* to his mother.

I *must have been painting* the house for days now.

I've been washing the dog. [The combination of perfect and progressive paints a vivid picture of a man deeply involved in a past process of some duration with immediate relevance to the wet present.]

4 The Adjective and the Adverb

Because the adjective and the adverb have so much in common, it is best to discuss them at the same time.

Adjectives and adverbs identify the distinctive feature of

something: the fastness of the horse in *the fast horse,* the fastness of the driving in *He drove fast,* the dishonor of the conduct in *dishonorable conduct,* the dishonor of the behaving in *He behaved dishonorably.*

4A Recognition of Adjectives and Adverbs

Adjectives and adverbs can be distinguished from each other by their form and their position in the sentence. Here are some ways of distinguishing these words.

(1) If a word fits one or both of the following blank positions, it is an adjective and not an adverb:

> He was very................ It was very................
>
> He was very *cowardly.* It was very *swampy.*
>
> *He was very *bravely.* [adverb]

Some adjectives, of course, will not fit these blanks because they should not be used with the intensifier *very.* (**He was very unique* is incorrect. Since *unique* means one of a kind, there are no real degrees of being *unique.*) More important, however, is the fact that other noun modifiers do not go in these blanks; therefore, this is a useful way to distinguish adjectives from other noun modifiers.

> *Because she was a *city* dweller, she was very *city.* [*City* can be a noun modifier, but it is not an adjective.]
>
> *Because it was a *gardening* tool, it was very *gardening.* [*Gardening* can be a noun modifier, but it is not an adjective.]
>
> Because he was a *jolly, green* giant, he was *green* and *jolly.* [*Green* and *jolly* are adjectives.]

(2) Adjectives and adverbs can sometimes be distinguished by form. Some of the several forms are listed below, including the most important one, which is that most adverbs are adjectives plus *ly.* (In a few cases both the adjective and the adverb end in *ly: cowardly, hourly.*)

	ADJECTIVE	ADVERB
theory [*noun*]	theoretical	theoretically
differ [*verb*]	different	differently
honor [*noun*]	honorable	honorably
coward [*noun*]	cowardly	cowardly
hour [*noun*]	hourly	hourly
collect [*verb*]	collective	collectively
back [*noun*]	backward	backward
shore [*noun*]		ashore
crab [*noun*]	crablike	crabwise

Recently, adverbs ending with *wise* have become popular, almost too popular because the reader may not be prepared for a particular noun's becoming an adverb. The following sentence should be avoided at present: *The Forty-niners did a remarkable job, special-teamwise.*

4B The Article

The most used adjectivals are the articles, *a, an,* and *the. A* and *an* are called indefinite articles because they single out any one unspecified member of a class. *The* is called a definite article because it specifies a particular member or a particular group of members of a class.

A is used when it immediately precedes a word beginning with a consonant sound: *a book, a tree. An* is used when it immediately precedes a word beginning with a vowel sound: *an apple, an ancient city.*

NOTE: It is the sound, not the actual letter, which determines the form of the indefinite article: *a university, an R.C.A. television set, an 8-sided object.* In some instances when there are different pronounciations of the same word, the pronounciation used by the speaker or writer determines the form of the article. If the writer pronounces the word *humble* omitting the aspirant or *h*-sound, then the form *an humble person* may be used.

4C Functions of Adjectives

While adjectives and adverbs can perform the same functions (verb complements and modifiers), their functions are usually quite distinct.

Adjectives modify a noun or function as the complements of copulative verbs such as **be, seem, feel.**

The *old* man, *tired* and *surly,* waited for the return of his children. [*Old, tired* and *surly* modify the noun *man.*]

I am *happy* that he feels *good.* [*Happy* and *good* are the complements of the verbs *be* and *feel.*]

4D Functions of Adverbs

Adverbs modify verbs and other modifiers.

He spoke to her *quietly.* [modifies the verb *spoke*]

She sang *extremely* well. [modifies the adverb *well*]

4E Comparison of Adjectives and Adverbs

Adjectives and adverbs have positive, comparative, and superlative forms. The positive form is the basic word: *small, beautiful, lush, loudly.*

For adjectives of one syllable, the comparative is usually formed by adding *er* to the positive form: *small, smaller; lush, lusher.* The superlative form of one-syllable adjectives is usually made by adding *-est* to the positive form: *small, smaller, smallest; lush, lusher, lushest.*

For most adjectives of more than one syllable and for most adverbs, the comparative and superlative are formed by combining *more* and *most* with the positive form: *beautiful, more beautiful, most beautiful; loudly, more loudly, most loudly.*

Some adjectives and adverbs do not follow these rules.

POSITIVE	COMPARATIVE	SUPERLATIVE
happy	happier	happiest
little	littler	littlest
bad	worse	worst
ill	worse	worst
good	better	best
well	better	best

Functions of Adjective and Adverb Comparison

The comparative form indicates a comparison of two things or two groupings of things. Usually the two things or groupings of things are mentioned explicitly in the sentence, but this is not always so.

She ran *faster* than her mother.

I've tasted *sweeter* raspberries than these.

After that restful night, he was *more relaxed* when we came to see him. [The comparison of two emotional states is implicit. The previous emotional state is implied, not stated.]

The superlative form is used when more than two things are compared.

She was the *fastest* reader in her family.

The *outermost* island was concealed by the approaching storm. [Other superlatives that end with *most* are *uppermost, innermost, westernmost, foremost,* etc.]

She shouted *the most loudly* of them all. [Some writers prefer to express the adverbial by means of an adjective form: *She shouted the loudest of them all.*]

4F   Confusion of Adjectives and Adverbs

Some words like *fast, slow, very, late* function as either adjectives or adverbs.

ADJECTIVE   It was a *fast* train. [modifies noun *train*]

ADJECTIVE   The clock was *fast*. [complements verb *was*]

ADVERB   The horse ran *fast*. [modifies verb *ran*]

The following adjectives and adverbs are sometimes confused: *good, well, bad, badly. Good* is an adjective and functions as an adjective.

He was a *good* man. [modifies noun *man*]

I feel *good*. [complements verb *feel*]

Well is an adjective meaning in good health and may be substituted for *good* in the preceding examples. But *well* is also an adverb meaning in a satisfactory or superior manner.

He played *well*. [modifies verb *played*]

He was *well* aware of his plight. [modifies adjective *aware*]

The adverb *badly* is sometimes mistaken for the adjective *bad*, meaning in poor spirits, in such sentences as *John feels bad, You look bad*. In both of these sentences, the adjective *bad* describes the condition of the subject (*John, you*). Never write: *I feel badly. He was badly mistaken* is correct.

When an adjective follows a copulative verb (like *is, feel, look, seem, become, smell*), it complements the verb and is known as a predicate adjective.

The water is (seems, feels, looks, is getting, is becoming) *hot*.

I feel (look, am) *fine, ill, sick, good, bad*.

You look *beautiful*. [not *beautifully*]

5   The Verbal

Verbals are verbs which have lost their subjects, their capacity to indicate definite time, and their capacity to express such ideas as necessity, obligation, and possibility.

5A   The Infinitive

The infinitive is the most versatile of the three verbals. It can be both active and passive, perfect and progressive.

> *To live* happily is not so hard. [present active form indicating present time]
>
> *To be living* today is not so bad. [present progressive active form indicating a continuous action in the present]
>
> He was pleased *to have been recommended.* [perfect passive form indicating two different times in the past]
>
> *To have been recommended* would have pleased him. [perfect passive form indicating that a past action could have happened, but didn't. This is a subjunctive use of the infinitive.]

The *to* in the infinitive is sometimes omitted. Compare: *Ask me to do it, Let me do it; He was made to confess, They made him confess.*

5B   The Present Participle

The name of this participle is misleading. It can indicate not only the present but also the past and the future.

> *Arriving* early, they smiled with embarrassment. [The actions are both in the past.]
>
> *Arriving* tomorrow, they will be met at the airport. [The actions are both in the future.]

The present participle has a perfect form in which the auxiliary **have** plus the -en or -ed form of the verb is used.

> *Having arrived* early, they decided to wait for their host. [The actions are at different times in the past.]

The Gerund

The gerund is a present participle that functions as a noun and therefore names an action or a state of being. Like the infinitive, it may have modifiers and complements.

> *Swimming* is good exercise.
>
> *Eating* too much is bad for one's health.
>
> *Being* gloomy was habitual to her.
>
> *Bowling* on the green was his favorite sport.

5C The Past Participle

The past participle can indicate past, present, and future meanings.

> Thus *deceived*, he will be outraged. [both actions in the future]
>
> *Baffled* by your attitude, I cannot help you. [both actions in the present]
>
> *Baffled* by your attitude, I could not help you. [both actions in the past]

The past participle has both perfect and progressive forms.

> *Having been discovered*, the thief confessed.
>
> *Being watched*, he could only pretend to mow the lawn.

5D Functions of Verbals

Because they have lost their subjects and their tense, verbals never function as do finite verbs. Instead, they function as nominals (structures that behave like nouns) or as modifiers.

Usually they carry along with them their own modifiers and verb completions.

When the present participle works as a nominal, it is called a **gerund**. The infinitive working as a nominal is still called an infinitive. Some of the more common uses of the verbal follow:

(1) *Verbals as nominals:*

Being watched made him nervous. [gerund as subject]

To be watched made him nervous. [infinitive as subject]

He was praised for his *typing*. [gerund as object of a preposition]

He urgently desired *to recant*. [infinitive as object of a verb]

(2) *Verbals as modifiers of nouns:*

His desire *to recant* was urgent. [modifies *desire*]

The *compromising* documents could not be found. [modifies *documents*]

The statement *typed* earlier that morning had been mislaid. [modifies *statement*]

(3) *Verbals as modifiers of verbs:*

He went to the mountains *to meditate*. [modifies *went*]

He scored his thousandth point *to lead* the league. [modifies *scored*]

(4) *Verbals as modifiers of adjectives:*

He was anxious *to cooperate*. [modifies *anxious*]

The man, eager *to see* what was going on, looked inside. [modifies *eager*]

To lead the league, *to see what was going on*, and *typed earlier that morning* are verbal phrases, that is, verbals with their modifiers and their verb completions.

6 Prepositions and Conjunctions

Prepositions and conjunctions are relationship words which are used to connect elements in the sentence. Relative pronouns have already been discussed in this context. Prepositions and the several kinds of conjunctions perform different functions and should be carefully distinguished from each other.

6A Recognition of Prepositions and Subordinating Conjunctions

Prepositions and subordinating conjunctions can be distinguished from each other by what follows them and by the fact that there are a limited number of subordinating conjunctions.

(1) *The preposition is followed by a nominal.* The nominal can be a noun, pronoun, gerund phrase, or noun clause.

> *because of* the bad weather [The noun *weather* is the object of the preposition *because of.*]
>
> *before* leaving home [The gerund phrase *leaving home* is the object of the preposition *before.*]
>
> *after* what he had done [The noun clause *what he had done* is the object of the preposition *after.*]

(2) *The subordinating conjunction is followed by a subject-verb structure with no other relationship word involved.* Thus *he had done* can follow a subordinating conjunction, and *what he had done* can follow a preposition.

> *because* the weather was bad [*Because* is a subordinating conjunction introducing the subordinate clause.]
>
> *before* he left home [*Before* is a subordinating conjunction introducing the subordinate clause.]

Before, after, since, as, until are both preposition and subordinating conjunction depending on what follows: *Since this morning; since you went away.*

(3) *"If," "when," "while," "although" and some others are subordinating conjunctions which can have their subject-verb structures transformed so that they begin to look like prepositional phrases.*

> When you were mopping the floor
> When mopping the floor
>
> If it is at all possible
> If at all possible
>
> although he was very angry
> although very angry

Because these conjunctions cannot easily take nouns after them (**when dinner*), they are being called conjunctions here, but it would be no great disaster if *when mopping the floor* were to be called a prepositional phrase.

(4) *Most prepositions and subordinating conjunctions by their function are not easily confused with each other.* The lists that follow are incomplete, but they do indicate the variety of structures that can be called prepositions and subordinating conjunctions.

PREPOSITIONS	SUBORDINATING CONJUNCTIONS
in	if
by	why
for	how
beneath	although
because of	because
in spite of	inasmuch as
considering [*verb form*]	provided that [*verb form*]
aboard [*adverb*]	who [*relative pronoun*]
except	that [*relative pronoun*]
than	that
as	than
	as

Despite the sustained campaign of advertising agencies, *like* is still a preposition in Standard American English.

Like I was saying, it's going to rain. [*As I was saying* is the preferred form.]

Like me, Hans enjoyed soccer.

*Samsons smell good *like* a walnut should. [*As a walnut should* is still preferred in the standard dialect.]

6B Coordinating Conjunctions

Coordinating conjunctions join sentence elements of equal importance. These conjunctions are *and, but, or, nor, for, yet.* They may join a word to another word (*bread and butter*), a phrase to another phrase (*into the oven or over the fire*), an independent clause to another independent clause (*He wanted to learn, but he hated to study*), a dependent clause to another dependent clause (*Matilda came in after I arrived but before dinner was served*).

Coordinating conjunctions are occasionally used effectively to introduce a sentence.

He said he would do it. *And* he did.

She swore that she told the truth. *Yet* she lied.

6C Correlative Conjunctions

Correlative conjunctions are pairs of words used to join sentence elements of equal importance. They are words like *both . . . and, either . . . or, neither . . . nor, not only . . . but also.* *Either* you go now, *or* you stay here forever. *Not only* was the team weak offensively, *but also* they were inept defensively.

7 Sentence Connectors

Sentence connectors join whole statements in clause or sentence form. Because some of these relationship words have adverbial forms (*obviously, naturally, unfortunately*), they are sometimes called **conjunctive adverbs**. The most common sentence connectors are *therefore, however, consequently, thus, then, in fact, moreover, nevertheless, so, in addition, meanwhile.* When they join independent clauses, they work with a semi-colon. When they relate sentences, a period is used.

> We watched his folly develop; *in fact*, we nurtured it.

> Joe Louis was a fantastically successful boxer. *However*, he did not emerge from his great career a rich man.

Unlike coordinating conjunctions, some sentence connectors can be inserted appropriately within the structure of the second statement.

> She was not pleased by his skating technique. She was delighted, *however*, by his self-control and poise.

8 The Interjection

Interjections (the word means *thrown in*) are words which do not fulfill any of the functions of the previous parts of speech. They are such words as *yes, no, oh, ah, well, hello.* Although they are frequently used in sentences, they are not properly parts of the sentence structure and are, therefore, separated from the remainder of the sentences by punctuation marks.

> *Oh*, I didn't see you.

> *Yes*, I'll do it.

> I waited, *alas*, too long.

> *No!* you can't mean it.

The Sentence and Its Parts

When we are speaking, our sentences can be quite short. One side of a telephone conversation will reveal things like "Yes . . . sure . . . why not . . . OK, about five o'clock." However, usually when we speak and always when we write, our sentences are longer, having a subject and a predicate.

9 The Subject and the Predicate

The sentence has two parts. The topic of the sentence is the **subject**. What is said about the subject is the **predicate**. Usually but not always, the subject identifies the agent of the action; that is, it tells us who or what is doing something.

SUBJECT	PREDICATE
The delegates	arrived this morning.
San Juan	is the capital of Puerto Rico.
Grambling, a small black college in Louisiana,	has produced many outstanding professional football players.

The city	was surrendered to Wallenstein.

[The subject of the sentence is *the city*, but the city didn't do anything. Something was done to the city by persons unspecified. The agent is not expressed in this sentence.]

The Positions of the Subject and the Predicate in the Sentence

Nearly always, the subject of the sentence comes first. There are occasions, however, when the subject does not come first.

(1) Occasionally for purposes of emphasis, the natural word order will be changed so that the predicate comes first.

Pete Rose roared into third base. [no emphasis]

Into third base roared Pete Rose. [emphasis on the predicate, which comes first]

(2) In sentences which ask questions rather than make statements, the subject can come first, but the more usual order is to place the subject inside the verb.

Your mother is coming today?

Is *your mother* coming today?

(3) In sentences which give commands rather than make statements, again the subject can come first, but, nearly always, the subject and part of the verb are deleted.

You will do as I tell you!

Do as I tell you!

(4) Sometimes, the subject can be moved out of its initial position, and a word that is lexically empty (that is, it has no meaning at all) takes its place.

To see you is nice. [*To see you* is the subject of the sentence.]

It is nice *to see you.* [*To see you* is still the subject of this sentence.]

Twelve players were on the field. [*Twelve players* is the subject of the sentence.]

There were *twelve players* on the field. [*Twelve players* is still the subject of the sentence. Moreover, because it is a plural subject, it makes the verb plural. Compare: There *was* one player on the field.]

9A Forms of the Subject

The subject of the sentence has several forms. The most frequent forms are nouns, proper nouns, and pronouns.

We shall overcome. [personal pronoun functioning as the subject]

Who is on third base? [interrogative pronoun functioning as the subject]

Marcus Garvey was a charismatic leader. [proper noun functioning as the subject of the sentence]

Those comments annoyed Jack. [noun functioning as the subject of the sentence]

Occasionally, larger structures, such as noun clauses, gerund phrases, and infinitive phrases, can function as the subject of a sentence. For convenience, nouns, pronouns, and these larger structures are called **nominals**.

What she did annoyed Jack. [noun clause functioning as the subject]

Playing chess amused Jack. [gerund phrase functioning as the subject]

To collect every stamp issued by Mexico was Juan's ambition. [infinitive phrase functioning as the subject]

(1) Simple and Complete Subjects

The noun or pronoun by itself is the **simple subject**. This subject is important to identify because it controls the form of the verb. The simple subject and the verb form it controls are in boldface type in these examples:

> **One** *of the ships* **is** sinking.
>
> *The* **mayor,** *as well as the councilmen,* **has** been implicated.

The noun phrase—that is, the noun and all its modifiers—is the **complete subject**. The complete subject (except for the boldface simple subject) is italicized in the examples above and below.

> *The* **furniture** *which they had bought on Monday* was delivered on Friday.

(2) The Compound Subject

Sometimes more than one nominal can be used as the subject of the sentence. The combination of several nominals to express the topic of the sentence is called a **compound subject**.

> *The* **drivers** *and the* **loaders** have threatened to strike.
>
> *Not only the* **price** *but also the* **quality** *of their products* fluctuates wildly.
>
> **What he did** *and* **what he said** were not the same.

9B Forms of the Predicate

The predicate, what is being said about the topic of the sentence, always has a verb. The verb usually has a verb completion called an **object** or a **complement**. Like the noun or the pronoun, the verb often has modifiers. The predicate of the sentence is, in effect, made up of a verb, a verb completion, and some verb modifiers. The various forms of the predicate depend on the kind of verb involved and the kind of verb completion.

(1) Predicate with a Transitive Verb

The most frequent form of the predicate is one where the verb expresses some kind of action and is followed by a nominal. This nominal is called the **object**; the verb is called a **transitive verb**.

In the following sentences the verbs *brought, tuned,* and *said* are transitive verbs. The nominals functioning as the objects of these verbs are italicized.

> They brought *their guitars* with them.
>
> Juanita tuned *the piano.*
>
> After the party Jack said *that they would have to clean the place.*

NOTE: Most transitive verbs must be completed by their objects. The following examples are not complete English sentences. (To show this, they are marked with an asterisk.)

> *They brought with them.
>
> *Juanita tuned.
>
> *After the party, Jack said.

Some transitive verbs can drop their objects and still make sense. *They have been celebrating* is as grammatical as *They had been celebrating his birthday.*

Some transitive verbs use two verb completions: a **direct object** and another structure called an **indirect object** or a **complement**, to refer to the object and complete the meaning of the verb. Both structures are needed to complete the thought. Compare:

*He gave his teacher.	He gave his *teacher* the *book.* [indirect object and direct object]
*The problem made Jack.	The problem made Jack *sweat.* [infinitive phrase *(to) sweat* as the complement]

(1) Nouns, pronouns and prepositional phrases starting with *to* or *for* can function as **indirect objects.**

Eliseo gave twenty pesos *to his brother*.

Eliseo gave *his brother* twenty pesos.

Luis cooked a meal *for his sister*.

Luis cooked *his sister* a meal.

He called *her* a taxi.

(2) Nouns, pronouns, prepositional phrases, adjectives, and verbal phrases can function as **complements.**

He called her a *star*. [The complement a *star* refers to the object *her*; they identify the same person. This can easily be confused with the two-object form above: *He called her a taxi.* (*You're a taxi* is not what is meant here!) A lot of bad television jokes are based on this confusion.]

He thought the whole thing *a bad joke*. [The noun *joke* and its modifiers function as the complement.]

They made her *taste the papaya*. [infinitive phrase *(to) taste the papaya* as the complement]

I made him *sick*. [adjective as the complement]

They heard their father *leaving the house*. [participle phrase as the complement]

He put the book *on the table*. [The prepositional phrase *on the table* functions as the complement. Note how essential it is to the sentence: **He put the book.*]

(2) Predicate with a Copulative Verb

When the verb expresses being, seeming, or becoming, the verb is called a **copulative verb**. These verbs are followed by a nominal, an adjective, or an adverbial. (An adverbial is anything that works like an adverb.)

Not many verbs function as copulatives, but those that do are common and are used frequently: *be, seem, become, remain, appear, look, feel, sound, taste, smell, grow*.

Puerto Rico became *a commonwealth* in 1952. [noun as complement]

Her point was *that Joe Louis was the greatest champion of all time.* [noun clause as complement]

Juanita will be *at her music teacher's house.* [The prepositional phrase is the complement. It is an adverbial telling where.]

The meat smelled *bad.* [The adjective is the complement. People sometimes use the adverb *badly* here. This is wrong. The copulative verb always takes an adjective rather than an adverb—even if it sounds bad!]

The careful use of adjectives after verbs marks one of the differences between standard and nonstandard usage. (Television commercials will deliberately use nonstandard forms, so do not trust them.) In standard usage, the adjective follows a copulative verb; very seldom does it follow transitive or intransitive verbs. Compare these uses:

*He played *good.*	He played *well.*
*This razor shaves *painless.*	This razor shaves *painlessly.*
*She sings *beautiful.*	She sings *beautifully.*

(3) Predicate with an Intransitive Verb

Some words do not need an object to complete them. These verbs can stand by themselves, or they are completed by an adverbial which indicates location or direction. The adverbial is called the **complement**. The verb, with or without the complement, is called an **intransitive verb**.

The situation deteriorated. [Nothing completes the verb; sometimes the symbol for "nothing" (φ) is used to indicate this.]

The clouds vanished φ. [Nothing completes the verb.]

He lay *down*. [The adverbial *down* completes the verb. Note: One cannot say **He lay*. This verb needs a complement to indicate where he lay.]

He sat *on the desk*. [The adverbial *on the desk* is the complement.]

(4) Compound Predicate Verbs and Verb Completions

Sometimes more than one verb or verb completion can occur in the predicate of the sentence. These structures are called the **compound verb**, the **compound object**, or the **compound complement**.

Their Puerto Rican heritage made *Luis* and *Rosita* proud. [two nouns functioning as the compound object]

Jack *fell* down and *broke* his crown. [two verbs functioning as the compound verb]

His stupid remark made her *angry* and *dangerous*. [two adjectives functioning as the compound complement]

9C   Phrases and Clauses

As we have seen already, words work together in groups which can be moved around as single units.

Someone had slashed *the furniture, which they had saved so hard for,* with a knife.

The furniture, which they had saved so hard for, had been slashed with a knife.

In the garden was a statue.

A statue was *in the garden*.

These moveable groups of words are called phrases and clauses. A brief listing of the word groups which are recognizable as particular kinds of phrases and clauses follows. Sometimes these word groups are recognizable because of their form, sometimes because of their function. All of these phrases and clauses have been mentioned in passing in previous sections.

(1) Phrases

Phrases are groups of words which do not have a subject and finite verb. Within them, however, can be inserted other structures which do have subjects and verbs.

(1) *A prepositional phrase* is a preposition followed by a nominal as its object. This phrase has too many functions to be of help in recognizing it.

> Stop *at the count of ten.* [The prepositional phrase has another prepositional phrase inside it and functions as a modifier of the verb *stop*.]
>
> The speaker was a woman *of extraordinary eloquence.* [The prepositional phrase modifies the noun woman.]
>
> He gave money *to whoever asked for it.* [The prepositional phrase has a clause with a subject and verb inside it. The phrase functions as an indirect object.]

(2) *A participle phrase* starts with a present or past participle. It modifies a noun or pronoun which is implicitly involved in the action expressed by the participle.

> *Holding the dog by its collar*, the boy refused to let go. [The participle phrase modifies *the boy*, the person holding the dog.]
>
> *Pulled tight across the frame*, the material looked more lustrous. [The participle phrase modifies *the material*, the substance which had been pulled tight.]
>
> He was a man *long admired for his patience.* [The

participle phrase modifies *a man*, the person who had been admired for a long time. Note that *long,* the modifier of the participle, comes before it.]

(3) *A gerund phrase* is a participle phrase which functions as a nominal.

Using profane language is not permitted here. [The gerund phrase is the subject of the verb *is permitted.*]

He caused the confusion by *suddenly changing lanes*. [The gerund phrase sits inside a prepositional phrase as the object of the preposition.]

(4) *An infinitive phrase* starts with an infinitive. Sometimes the **to** of the infinitive form is omitted. This phrase has too many functions to be of help in recognizing it.

It was our desire *to serve humanity*. [The infinitive phrase functions as the subject of *was.*]

I have a bone *to pick with you*. [The infinitive phrase modifies *bone.*]

He wanted *to see if the young birds had left the nest*. [The infinitive phrase is the object of *wanted*. It has inside it a clause with a subject and verb.]

We watched the bird *feed its young*. [The infinitive phrase is the objective complement of the verb *watched.*]

(5) *A noun phrase* is a noun with its determiner and its modifiers. It is the noun phrase, not the noun, which is usually replaced by a pronoun.

The furniture, which they had saved so hard for, had been slashed with a knife. There was no doubt that *it* had been irretrievably ruined. [The noun phrase is the noun, its determinant *the*, and the relative clause modifying *furniture.*]

His best six young black and white grazing dairy cows in the lower field which have not yet been milked are getting noisy. [This artificial example is presented here to show that a noun phrase can have a considerable number of noun modifiers in it.]

(6) *A verb phrase* is not easy to define, because grammarians cannot agree on what to recognize as a verb phrase. There are at least three different patterns currently in use. Here we will describe the verb phrase as a main verb and its auxiliaries: She *could have been watching* him.

(2) Clauses

Clauses are groups of words which have subjects and finite verbs. Usually clauses are introduced by such relationship words as *who, that, so that, where, but, and, however.* Clauses can stand by themselves, or they can be dependent on other structures.

Independent Clauses

An independent clause can stand by itself. In this case, it starts with a capital letter and ends with a period (.), a question mark (?), or an exclamation point (!). It is called a sentence.

Hold tight!   She's pretty.   Who did it?

An independent clause can be joined to another independent clause by punctuation, coordinating conjunctions, or sentence connectors.

Mrs. Butler spends lavishly; she has an independent income; unfortunately, she has no taste.

An independent clause can work with dependent clauses and can have dependent clauses inserted within itself.

When she got there, *she discovered that the cupboard was bare.* [The independent clause has inside it a dependent clause functioning as the object of the transitive verb.]

Dependent Clauses

Like phrases, dependent clauses function as nominals and as modifiers. A dependent clause can be sometimes recognized by its introductory relationship word. A clause starting with *because* is always an adverb clause. Equally often, however, a dependent clause has to be recognized by its function in the sentence. A clause starting with *that* can be a noun clause, an adjective clause, or an adverb clause. Only its use in a particular sentence can identify it.

(1) *Noun clauses* usually start with *that*, but they can start with relative pronouns like *who* or *what*, or they can start with subordinating conjunctions like *if, when, why, where,* or *how*. Noun clauses function as nominals.

> They hoped *that the war would end soon.* [object of the verb *hoped*]
>
> *How he escaped* was stated in the report. [subject of the verb *was stated*]
>
> Knowing *who was cheating* disturbed him greatly. [object of the participle *knowing*]
>
> They made it clear *he should pay immediately.* [objective complement of the verb *made*. Note that the conjunction *that* has been deleted from the dependent clause.]

(2) *Adjective clauses* nearly always start with relative pronouns, although these pronouns are sometimes deleted. When the noun antecedent refers to a place or a time, the adjective clause can begin with the subordinating conjunctions *where* or *when*. Adjective clauses modify nouns and pronouns and follow them as closely as possible.

> A man *I know* grows tomato plants *that never bear fruit.* [The adjective clauses modify *man* and *plants*. As these clauses identify which man and which plants are being talked about, they are called **restrictive clauses** and are left unpunctuated.]

He spoke to the woman in the car *who was drinking a can of soda.* [modifies the noun *woman*]

My brother, *who is not very sentimental,* did visit the Moravian village *where we were born.* [The first adjective clause is set off by commas to indicate that it is **nonrestrictive**; that is, it gives additional information rather than restricting the meaning of the noun.]

(3) *Adverb clauses* start with a variety of subordinating conjunctions which usually indicate such meanings as time, place, reason, manner, condition, etc. Adverb clauses function as modifiers of verbs, other modifiers, and sentences.

He was bitter *that she had deserted him.* [modifies the adjective *bitter*]

We should answer *when she calls.* [modifies the verb *should answer*]

As she turned to go, she smiled at him. [modifies the verb *smiled*]

As I have stated before, the cupboard was indeed bare. [modifies the sentence itself]

9D Classification of Sentences by Clause Type

For easy reference, a sentence can be classified according to the distribution of independent and dependent clauses. A **simple sentence** is an independent clause (*Facts are stubborn things*). A **compound sentence** has two or more independent clauses (*There the wicked cease from troubling, and the weary be at rest*). A **complex sentence** has an independent clause and one or more dependent clauses (*When she got there, the cupboard was bare*). A **compound-complex sentence** has two or more independent clauses and one or more dependent clauses (*Jack fell down, and Jill came tumbling after because she was too busy watching Jack*).

9E   Modification

As has been shown in previous sections, subjects, objects, complements, and finite verbs are the basic elements which work together to make up the sentence. **Modifiers**, on the other hand, depend on other structures for their existence in the sentence. In the first example below, the adjective *old* is the complement of the verb. In the second example, the meaning of *old* stays the same, but its function has changed. The adjective *old* now depends on, and is subordinate to, the noun *man*.

> The man is *old*. [adjective as complement]
>
> The *old* man is tired. [adjective as modifier of the noun *man*]
>
> The apartment *upstairs* was available. [adjective as modifier of the noun *apartment*]
>
> The apartment I wanted was *upstairs*. [adverb as complement]
>
> Someone was playing drums *upstairs*. [adverb as modifier of the verb *was playing*]

(1)   Modifiers of Verbs

Verb modifiers identify the distinctive features of the action or state of being expressed by the finite verb or the verbal. The modifiers tell where, when, why, how, how often, how much, with what results, under what circumstances or conditions something occured.

The structures most frequently used as verb modifiers or **adverbials**, as they are sometimes called, are adverbs, nouns, prepositional phrases, infinitive phrases, and adverb clauses.

> *When he spoke,* they fell silent. [adverb clause of time modifying *fell*]
>
> They went to Carnegie Hall *to hear Marian Anderson sing*. [infinitive phrase of cause modifying *went*]

Verb modifiers *frequently* occur *after the verb.* [adverb of frequency and prepositional phrase of place modifying *occur*]

Delighted *because she had arrived early*, he opened the champagne. [adverb clause of cause modifying the verbal *delighted*]

They arrived *this morning.* [noun of time modifying *arrived*]

(2) Position of Verb Modifiers

Most verb modifiers can move around the sentence without changing their function or meaning: *He raised his hand slowly; Slowly he raised his hand; He slowly raised his hand.* A few verb modifiers do not move so easily: *He arrived early;* *Early he arrived;* *He early arrived.*

(3) Modifiers of Nouns

Noun modifiers are divided into those that are noun markers or **determiners** and those which identify distinctive features in nouns and are called **adjectivals**.

(4) Determiners

Determiners are noun modifiers which express large general features such as definiteness, indefiniteness, quantity, countableness, singularity, plurality. The most common determiners are articles (*the, a, an*), demonstrative pronouns (*this, those*), personal pronouns (*my, his*), and noun possessives (*Ramon's, the child's*).

These determiners exclude each other. If one is used, the other can't be: *the my chicken,* *that his book,* *the this curfew.* (It is possible to say *this, the curfew*, but, here, *this* is not a determiner.)

Other pronouns can function as determiners, and some of them can work together (*all my joys*). Some examples of single and multiple determiners follow below:

> *some* examples [an indefinite countable number of examples]
>
> *both the boys* [two definite countable boys]
>
> *much* courage [an uncountable amount of courage]
>
> *we* Americans [several definite Americans associated with the speaker]
>
> *you* children [several definite children]
>
> *five books* [a countable number of indefinite books]
>
> *five of the books* [a countable number of definite books]
>
> *Ramon's* few enemies [an indefinite number of countable enemies possessed by Ramon]

Some other words which work as determiners are as follows: *other, many, another, any, several, more, most, first, last, second, third, enough, no, which, all, each, neither, either.*

(5) Adjectivals

Adjectivals are noun modifiers which identify a large number of distinctive features in the nouns they modify. These distinctive features can range from such things as the ability to be parked in (as in *the parking lot*) to such things as physical condition, age, weather involvement, religious posture, and identity (as in *the tired, old, rain-drenched, blasphemous man whom men called Lear*).

The structures most frequently used as adjectivals are adjectives, nouns, adverbs, prepositional phrases, participle phrases, infinitive phrases, and relative clauses.

(6) Position of Adjectivals

Most adjectivals have a fixed position in the word order. They cannot move freely.

The pretty child	*the child pretty
The man, angry at his daughter	*the angry at his daughter man
the filled parking lot	*the parking filled lot

a. Short adjectivals, with the exception of adverbs, sit between the determiner and the noun. Determiner and noun are given in boldface in the following examples.

the wounded marine **sergeant**

a tall, dark, distinguished **gentleman**

the beautiful red **dress**

the stimulating, intelligent **conversation** afterwards

the French language **teacher**

NOTE: There can be ambiguity when an adjective is followed by two nouns. In the preceding example, the teacher could be a Frenchman teaching German or someone of unspecified nationality who teaches the French language.

---

b. Most longer adjectivals come after the noun they modify because they are derived from a sentence which is inserted after the noun. This sentence or clause repeats the noun and usually uses the verb **be.**

*Abdul-Jabbar—Abdul-Jabbar is the greatest basketball player today—played a quiet, methodical game.

To make the sentence grammatical, the inserted sentence is kept by replacing the repeated noun with a relative pronoun—to produce an adjectival relative clause.

Abdul-Jabbar, who is the greatest basketball player today, played a quiet, methodical game.

A second solution is to reduce the sentence to a phrase by deleting the repeated noun and the part of the verb **be**.

> Abdul-Jabbar, the greatest basketball player today, played a quiet, methodical game. [The noun phrase following *Abdul-Jabbar* is an adjectival modifying *Abdul-Jabbar*. It is sometimes called an **appositive**.]

The following inserted sentences are transformed into various adjectivals which come after the noun they modify.

> *that car—that car is in the parking lot . . . that car *in the parking lot* [prepositional phrase]
>
> *the car—the car was sold yesterday . . . the car *sold yesterday* [past participle phrase]
>
> *the car—the car was to be sold tomorrow . . . the car *to be sold tomorrow* [infinitive phrase]
>
> *our car—our car was boiling gently . . . our car, *boiling gently* [present participle]

Participle phrases can move out of the position after the noun: *boiling gently, our car . . . .* In this situation the participle phrase can sometimes lose track of the noun it modifies and can "dangle." (See Section 17.)

(7) Modifiers of Adjectives and Adverbs

Adjectives and adverbs are often modified by adverbs which indicate the comparative intensity of the quality involved. A man can be *slightly* tired, *somewhat* tired, or *very* tired. These adverbs are called **intensifiers.**

> She spoke *quite* firmly to him. [adverb somewhat intensified]
>
> He was *rather* quiet when she spoke. [adjective somewhat intensified]

She was *extremely* happy to see him. [adjective very intensified]

He was a *little* depressed. [adjective slightly intensified]

As a result, they sang *much* more loudly. [adverb very intensified]

Quite a few words function as intensifiers, some polite and some indelicate. Every dialect has its favorite, sometimes faddish, intensifiers. Unless you are a Texan or an affected Englishman, do not write that you are *mighty* pleased or *frightfully* pleased to see your friends. In writing, *real* pleased and *sure* pleased are also dialect forms to be avoided.

(8) Large Structure Modifiers of Adjectives and Adverbs

Certain adverbs like *so, more, such, as*, and a few adjectives like *glad, happy, disappointed, bitter, conscious, aware, similar, different* can be modified by large structures such as the prepositional phrase and the adverb clause starting with the subordinating conjunctions *that, than,* and *as*.

a. When "so," "more," "such," and "as" modify an adjective, they usually require an adverb clause to indicate the nature of the comparison or the result involved. The adverb clause is dependent on the adverb, not the adjective. Remove the adverb, and the adverb clause cannot stand after the adjective. **He was tired that he couldn't stand up.* [should be *so tired that*]

He was *so* glad to see her *that he jumped over the sofa.*

They had *such* bad weather *that they left after a week.*

He was *as* angry *as he had ever been.*

He was *more* upset *than she had expected.*

b. Some adjectives require a completion in a way that certain verbs do. It was ugly is a complete statement; *it was similar* sounds incomplete. These "transitive" adjectives usually take a prepositional phrase or an adverb clause starting with *that*. These large structures are the modifiers of the adjective. (One or two grammarians are now calling them the "object" of the adjectives.)

He was aware *of his weakness*.

He was aware *that he had a weakness*.

She was happy *about his buying the car*.

She was happy *that he had bought the car*.

She was happy *to see him*.

It was similar *to the others*.

He was different *from the other boys*.

Like some transitive verbs, some of these adjectives can stand by themselves without their modifiers. *He was devious, calculating, and bitter. After the catastrophe, she was happy.*

Sentence Errors

A knowledge of words, phrases, clauses, basic structures, modification, and agreement is essential to good writing, but such a knowledge does not guarantee that our first drafts will not be confused and marred by writing errors. When we are thinking of several things at once and alternate wordings go racing through the mind, it is all too easy to write inaccurately. The painstaking correction of writing errors is an inevitable part of good writing. Only after this process of correction is completed by the writer can the reader concentrate on what we are saying rather than on how we are saying it.

In early drafting, whole sentences can go awry. To enable the reader to concentrate on the content of the material, the writing must contain complete, separate sentences. Fused sentences, comma faults, and sentence fragments are the sentence errors that most severely dislocate the continuity of the writing.

10 Sentence Fragments

10A Recognition of Sentence Fragments

When modifiers or nominals are lengthy, careless writers will sometimes allow them to break off from their sentences to stand by themselves. The modifier or nominal left standing alone is called a sentence fragment.

In the following example, an adverb clause is left standing by itself. *Because he was serving his residency at the overcrowded city hospital. The reader is left in suspense, asking, "Well, what about it?" The writer may add a new sentence: He had little leisure time, but this is not a good repair job. The fragment still stands.

10B The Correction of Sentence Fragments

Sentence fragments can be corrected in two ways:

(1) by properly relating the large modifier to its noun or verb or relating the large nominal to its verb.

(2) by starting all over again and converting the modifier or nominal into a sentence which can stand by itself.

Below are examples of sentence fragments and illustrations of one or both methods of repair.

FRAGMENT adverb clause as modifier	*While millions of people all over the world are dying of starvation.
CORRECTION by first method	We have an abundance of food while millions of people all over the world are dying of starvation. [adverb clause modifier of *have*]
FRAGMENT infinitive phrase as modifier	*To hear Beethoven's piano sonatas played by a great pianist.
CORRECTION by first method	We went to Royce Hall yesterday evening to hear Beethoven's

piano sonatas played by a great pianist. [infinite phrase modifier of *went*]

FRAGMENT
participle
phrase as
modifier

*Believing in equal opportunity for all.

CORRECTION by
second method

My Congresswoman believed in equal opportunity for all. Therefore she was a strong advocate of a good civil rights bill. [verbal *believing* transformed into a finite verb *believed*]

FRAGMENT
gerund phrase

*Giving an aggressive nation whatever it demands.

CORRECTION by
first method

I do not advocate giving an aggressive nation whatever it demands. [gerund phrase object of *do not advocate*]

FRAGMENT
noun phrase as
modifier (ap-
positive)

*A brilliant, hard-driving man who will not tolerate slackness.

CORRECTION by
first method

The greatest influence on my life has been my Uncle Oscar, a brilliant, hard-driving man who will not tolerate slackness. [noun phrase modifier of *Uncle Oscar*]

CORRECTION by
second method

Uncle Oscar is a brilliant, hard-driving man who will not tolerate slackness. He also happens to be the greatest influence on my life. [noun phrase transformed back to original copulative sentence]

11 The Comma Fault

When the writer uses a comma between two sentences, rather than relating them with a semicolon or a relationship word or separating them with a period, space, and capital letter, the result is called a comma fault or comma splice and can sometimes be confusing.

> *Classes will begin on September 19, the year 1984 should be a good one for all of us at Northern State.

Sometimes it is more obvious what the writer intends to say.

> *We had taken the wrong turning, we found we were heading south instead of west.

The comma fault is easily repaired by making two sentences out of the spliced sentences. *Classes will begin on September 19. The year 1984 should be a good one for all of us at Northern State.* If this solution seems too abrupt, then one of the methods of coordinating two sentences should be employed.

> We had taken the wrong turning, *and* we found we were heading south instead of west. [coordinating conjunction *and* punctuated with a comma]

> We had taken the wrong turning; we found we were heading south instead of west. [semicolon relating two sentences with similar content]

> We had taken the wrong turning; *thus* we found we were heading south instead of west. [sentence connector *thus* punctuated with a semiolon]

12 The Fused Sentence

The fused sentence is two or more sentences run together with no punctuation or spacing to separate them. As a result, the reader, misled and confused, must reread the sentence and, even then, may not always catch the writer's intent.

> *With gladness, we see the Christmas season approach
> Mrs. Dunkeld and I share our joy with you.

The quick cure for the fused sentence is to make two distinct sentences out of it.

> With gladness, we see the Christmas season approach.
> Mrs. Dunkeld and I share our joy with you.

If the two sentences sound awkward, then the use of relationship words such as coordinating conjunctions and sentence connectors may be in order.

> With gladness we see the Christmas season approach.
> Mrs. Dunkeld and I, therefore, share our joy with you.

Logic and Clarity

The basic structures and modifiers of a sentence are bound together by meaning, relationship words, and word order. Another way of making the elements of a sentence cohere is the relating of significant forms. This relating of forms is called agreement.

13 Agreement of Subject and Verb

Agreement occurs when a structure changes its form because of the influence of another structure. In English, nominal subjects influence the forms of finite verbs; nominals also influence the forms of pronouns. In some European languages, a noun will influence the form of the article that comes before it. Thus in Spanish we find *la televisión* and *el fútbol: la* is used because the noun is feminine; *el* is used because the noun is masculine. In English, distinctions are occasionally based on gender, but number is the most common ground on which agreement is based.

13A Subject and Verb Agreement by Number

The rule for number agreement is not difficult. A singular subject requires a singular verb; a plural subject requires a plural verb. To apply the rule, however, you must be able to do three things: remember that the subject controls the verb form and not be distracted by other structures which may stand close to the verb; be able to determine the number of the subject; and finally, know the correct singular and plural forms of the verb.

13B   Selection of the Subject to Control the Number of the Verb Form

In the sentence *One of our ships is missing* there is a temptation to let the plural noun *ships,* which stands by the verb, control the verb form because *ships is* sounds peculiar. The temptation must be resisted, for it is the more remote word *one,* the subject of the verb, which controls the number of the verb. There are several circumstances where another structure may distract the writer from remembering that the subject controls the number of the verb form.

(1) *The verb agrees with the subject, not with the elements in the modifier of the subject.*

> *Each* of the sofas *is* ninety inches long.
>
> A *swarm* of bees *is* coming towards us.
>
> The *men* in the district office *have* organized a ball team. [*Sofas, bees,* and *office* stand close to the verb, but they do not control the form of the verb; the subject does.]

(2) *The verb agrees with the subject even if the following modifier sounds and looks like a coordinator joining two nouns.* Several prepositions have a strong coordinating sense, such as *including, together with, along with, no less than, in addition to,* and *as well as,* but the verb that follows must agree with the noun subject that is modified by the prepositional phrase.

> The *mayor,* as well as the councilmen, *has* been implicated. [*Mayor* is the singular subject which controls the form of the singular verb *has been implicated*]

(3) *The verb agrees with the subject, not with the following complement.*

> The greatest *nuisance is* the refunds we have to make.

> The *children* of today *are* the hope of tomorrow. [The complement nouns *refunds* and *hope* do not control the verb form. To do so, they must be moved into the subject position of the sentence to become the subjects of their sentences: The *hope* of tomorrow *is* the children of today.

(4) *If for any reason the subject is moved out of the subject position, it will still control the verb form as long as another nominal is not moved into its place.*

> *Ramon and Eduardo are* at the jai alai game.

> Where *are Ramon and Eduardo?* [The sentence has been transformed into a question, and *Ramon and Eduardo* is still the subject of the sentence.]

> There *were twelve players* on the field. [*There* has been moved into the subject position, but it means nothing; it is an expletive, a space-filler, and *twelve players* is still the subject of the sentence as is *a fight* in the sentence *There was a fight on the field.* The subjects control the verb forms.]

There is one exception to the rule. The word *it* also can function as an expletive displacing the subject of the sentence. However, because it is also a singular pronoun, it controls the verb even if the subject is plural.

> *It is* ambitious executives who catch the early train. [*Ambitious executives* is the plural subject, but it is the expletive *it* which controls the verb form *is.*]

Usually the subject displaced by *it* is obviously singular so that it doesn't really matter what controls the singular verb form.

> It is rumored *that he is about to resign.* [The noun clause is the singular subject of the sentence.]

13C Selection of the Correct Number of the Noun Subject to Control the Verb Form

Most problems in subject-verb agreement occur because the number of the noun or nouns functioning as the subject is not always apparent. *The fish* can be singular or plural despite its singular form. *The news* is always singular despite its plural form.

(1) *Some nouns in the plural form can be singular in meaning, or they can be plural in meaning.* Trousers, tongs, wages, tactics, pliers, scissors, odds and barracks are plural in meaning. Therefore they require a plural verb.

The scissors *are* in the lefthand drawer.

Billiards, news, mathematics, linguistics, mumps, and *measles* are singular in meaning. Therefore they require a singular verb.

Measles *is* a communicable disease. [Some people do say, however, that *Measles are catching.*]

(2) *Some nouns in the plural form can be both singular and plural.* When they denote fields of knowledge or activity, they are singular; in most other uses, they are plural.

Politics *has* always attracted persons of talent.

The politics of the situation *are* complicated.

Statistics *is* not always a dry subject.

The statistics *were* largely erroneous.

(3) *Some nouns which specify an amount of something are singular when the things or people involved are regarded as a unit.* In this case, they take a singular verb.

Two plus two *is* four.

Two-thirds of the sweater *has* been completed.

Eight pounds of grapes *seems* a lot.

Ten percent of their capital *has* been absorbed already.

Ten percent of the men drafted *are* over thirty. [Here the men are regarded as individuals, not as a unit.]

(4) *Collective nouns are usually singular but can be plural.* If the collective is regarded as a unit, the collective noun is singular and requires a singular verb.

> The orchestra *performs* well under any conductor.

> The family *is* coming over this afternoon.

If, however, members of the collective are considered individually, the collective noun is plural and requires a plural verb.

> The family *were* informed as soon as they could be reached by telephone. [Members of the family were informed individually by means of several telephone calls.]

(5) *The number of some foreign plurals can be confused where a plural is mistaken for a singular.*

> *The public media *is* in trouble. [*Media* is plural in form and meaning; therefore the verb should be plural. *The public media are in trouble.*]

> *This phenomena *fascinates* him. [*These phenomena fascinate him.*]

13D Selection of the Correct Number of the Compound Subject to Control the Verb Form

(1) *A compound subject coordinated by "and" is nearly always plural and requires a plural verb form.*

> Mink and sable *are* expensive furs.

> The senator and his wife *were* warmly received.

If, however, the compound subject refers to just one person or thing, then the verb form is singular.

> A scholar and a gentleman *is* what he strives to be. [one person]

> This prelude and fugue *is* by Bach. [one composition]

When the compound subject refers to closely related things, it can be singular or plural depending on the closeness of the relationship. In borderline cases, the singular form of the following verb sounds better.

> The courage and patriotism of De Gaulle *were* cherished by many Frenchmen in 1940. [The two qualities are related but distinct from each other; so the plural verb form is used.]

> The protection and feeding of young fledglings *is* the constant preoccupation of the adult birds. [The two qualities seem so close that the singular verb form is used.]

(2) *Singular nouns coordinated by "or," "either . . . or," "neither . . . nor," or by "not only . . . but also" are regarded as a singular subject and require a singular verb form.*

> Not only the mother but also the child *was* badly dehydrated.

> Either the muffler or the tailpipe *was* replaced.

> Neither time nor prosperity *has* softened his heart.

> I think Armando or Helen *has* our passports.

When these coordinating conjunctions join plural nouns, the verb is plural. (*Neither the Saints nor the Packers are going to win this year.*) When these conjunctions join singular and plural nouns, then the verb agrees in number with the closer noun to it.

> Neither his advisors nor the President himself *has* acted wisely in this crisis. [*President* is closer to the verb.]

> Either the cloth or the dyes *are* defective. [*Dyes* is closer to the verb.]

Some writers dislike this construction and recast the sentence to avoid it.

> Either the cloth *was* defective or the dyes *were*.

13E Selection of the Correct Number of the Pronoun Subject to Control the Verb Form

(1) *Most indefinite pronouns are regarded as singular pronouns and require a singular verb form.*

> *Somebody* across the street *is* playing a trombone.
>
> As yet *nobody has* challenged my theory.
>
> *Each* of the sofas *is* over ninety inches long. [The singular pronoun *each,* not the plural noun *sofas* controls the verb form.]
>
> *Everybody* in the room *was* getting sleepy. [Despite the fact that *everybody* is obviously plural in meaning, it is a singular pronoun in the standard dialect.]

Some of these indefinite pronouns can work as determiners before singular nouns, and although there may be a strong feeling that more than one thing is involved, the verb form is still singular.

> Neither idea *was* any good. [Although the speaker is talking about two ideas being no good, in the standard dialect the verb form must be singular.]
>
> Each baby chick *was* inspected to establish its sex. [Thousands of chicks were probably being processed this way, but the singular noun *chick* and the singular meaning of *each* demand that the verb be singular in form.]

(2) *A few indefinite pronouns such as "many," "several," and "few" refer to more than one person or thing.* These pronouns are plural and take plural verb forms.

> Several *have* already been tested.
>
> Many *are* called, but few *are* chosen.

The nouns *variety* and *number* also take plural verb forms when they are preceded by *a*. When they are preceded by *the*, they are singular.

> *A* variety of fish *abound* in these waters.
>
> *A* number of horsemen *were* on the hill.
>
> *The* number of horsemen on the hill *was* not great.

(3) *Like collective nouns, some indefinite pronouns can be either singular or plural depending on whether they refer to a quantity or individual units of something.*

> Some of the cereal *is* wormy. [a quantity of cereal]
>
> Some of the apples *are* rotten. [several individual apples]
>
> Most of the money *is* gone; so *are* most of the people. [A quantity of money and several people have disappeared.]

The pronoun *none* behaves in a similar fashion; in addition, it can be singular when the meaning of *not one* of the individuals is intended.

> Luckily, *none* of the property *was* damaged; *none* of the horses *were* hurt; but *none* of us *is* blameless in this matter.

(4) *A relative pronoun can be either singular or plural depending on the number of its antecedent. Sometimes the antecedent is not easy to find.*

> She is one of those courageous *women who have* sacrificed their lives for woman's rights. [*Who* can refer in general for its meaning to *she, one,* or *women*. Specifically it refers to the plural *women*. Therefore the verb that the pronoun *who* controls is plural.]

13F Selection of the Correct Form of the Verb to Agree with the Subject by Number

Singular and plural verb forms are usually not hard to identify. The correct form means, in this context, that form which is used in Standard American English. Many dialects of English use other forms which are correct in these dialects but are wrong if they are used in Standard American English. Below are some verb forms which are correct in their dialects but should not be employed when using Standard American English.

> *He *don't* know what he's doing. [*Don't* is the correct third person singular form in many English dialects. The correct form in Standard American English is *doesn't*. *Doesn't* must always be used in the standard dialect. *He doesn't know what he is doing.*]

> *They *be* doing that all the time. [*Be* is the correct third person plural form in some black American dialects and in some British English dialects. The correct form in the standard dialect is *are*. *They are doing that all the time.*]

> *I'm right, *amn't I?* [*Amn't* is the correct first person singular form in some Scottish dialects. *Ain't* is the correct form in several American and British dialects, but the correct standard singular form is the plural form *aren't*. *I'm right, aren't I?* This does not make a lot of sense, but one must remember that language usage is not always logical.]

13G Subject-Verb Agreement by Person

In English, the person of the subject noun or pronoun has little effect on the form of the verb. Only one verb **be** has several forms which change in accord with the first, second and third persons of pronouns: *I am, you are, she is, I was, you were.* Some auxiliary verbs are unchanged by the person of the subject: *I can, you can,* *she can.* All other verbs change only in relation to the third person singular of the present tense: *I talk, he talks.* This change is not observed in all dialects of English, but Standard American English demands a distinction between the two forms. **The man talk all night* is a serious error.

14 Agreement of Pronoun and Antecedent

As was pointed out in Section 2, a pronoun is a word which sometimes lacks specific meaning. Most pronouns depend on another structure for their meaning. The other structure, the antecedent, controls the pronoun as regards number, person, gender, and the lexical features of people and things. Some of the pronouns which are controlled by their antecedents are the personal, demonstrative, and relative pronouns.

14A Selection of the Correct Pronoun Based on the Number of the Antecedent

(1) *Collective nouns can be singular or plural depending on whether the collective or the several individuals involved are emphasized.* The following pronoun will be singular or plural accordingly.

> The staff expressed *its* confidence in *its* medical director. [The staff acted collectively.]

> The staff have been airing *their* grievances publicly. [Individual staff members had been complaining.]

> The committee submits *its* report annually.

> He ordered the committee to cease *their* bickering. [Many writers find this construction artificial and will insert the

plural word *members* after *committee* to accommodate the plural pronoun *their.*]

NOTE: As regards gender, collective nouns are neuter, requiring the pronouns *it, its* and *which.*

(2) *Indefinite pronouns are usually singular but can be plural depending on whether a quantity or individual units are emphasized.* The following pronoun will be singular or plural accordingly.

> *Some* of the cereal has kept *its* freshness, but *some* of the apples have worms in *their* cores. [The cereal is in quantity, the apples in individual units.]
>
> *Neither* idea had any point to *it.*
>
> *Each* of the sofas has lost *its* castors.
>
> *Everybody* raised *his or her* voice in song. [Occasionally the plural sense is so strong that some writers are tempted to use a plural pronoun. *Everybody grabbed their coats and ran.*]

NOTE: As regards gender, the masculine pronoun has traditionally been used to refer to an indefinite pronoun (like *everyone*); today, however, *his or her* is considered the preferred form to use when an indefinite pronoun is the antecedent: *Everyone is wearing his or her jogging suit to the picnic.* (See also Section 14B.)

(3) *A compound subject is singular when the coordinator is "or" and plural when the coordinator is "and."*

> The senator and his wife were warmly received after *their* world tour.
>
> Either Vincente or Martin may leave *his* children with us.

When one of the antecedents joined by *or* or *nor* is plural, the pronoun agrees in number with the closer antecedent.

Neither the producer nor the *sponsors* admit *they* were aware of the fraudulent practices.

Neither the sponsors nor the *producer* admits that *he* was aware of the fraudulent practices.

(4) *When the antecedent of the pronoun is a large structure like a sentence, the following pronoun is always singular.*

Lumsden tried to calm the child's fears. He found *this* more difficult than he had expected. [Some writers are unhappy about a pronoun taking the place of a sentence and will insert a noun in order to avoid using a pronoun in this manner. *He found this activity more difficult than he had expected.*]

14B Selection of the Correct Pronoun Based on the Person and Gender of the Antecedent

As nearly all noun and pronoun antecedents are third person, there is seldom any problem in selecting the correct pronoun to follow them. *Mr. Riggs said that* **he** *would accept the chairmanship.* On rare occasions a second person pronoun will follow the name of a person. *Mr. Riggs,* **you** *come down here at once!*

As far as gender is concerned, English bases gender on sexual difference, whereas other European languages use arbitrary gender distinctions where football is masculine, television is feminine, and a girl can be neuter. In English, a masculine pronoun follows a male antecedent; a feminine pronoun follows a female antecedent; and a neuter pronoun follows nearly all other antecedents. Thus *a girl* is *she, an uncle* is *he,* and *a comb* is *it.*

Traditionally, masculine pronouns have been used to refer to abstract, singular nouns like *mayor, judge, professor, doctor, senator, employer, person,* and *reader:*

A judge must use *his* discretion in such a matter.

Since, today, women have assumed larger roles in many formerly masculine fields, the problem of "sexist" language arises. It can be solved in several ways:

(1) by using both third person singular pronouns

A judge must use *his or her* discretion in such a matter.

(2) by using plural forms to avoid the singular human noun

Judges must use *their* discretion in such matters.

(3) by alternating masculine and feminine pronouns throughout the material

(4) by the sparing use of *you*

Once the writer has determined his purpose . . .

Once *you* have determined *your* purpose . . .

(5) by revising the sentence

(a) The worker should divide his task . . .

The task should be divided . . .

(b) If the beginner is guided by these rules, he should be . . .

The beginner guided by these rules should be . . .

14C   Selection of the Correct Pronoun Based on the Antecedent Being Human or Nonhuman

It and *its* are the pronouns used when the antecedent is nonhuman. However, animals whose sex is significant or who are well-known to the speaker can be called *he* or *she*, which are the pronouns used for antecedents which are human.

The relative pronouns *who, whom, that* refer to antecedents which are human (or are familiar animals); *which, that* refer to antecedents which are nonhuman.

> He is one of *those who* know all too well that the *memories which* move us fade all too fast. [*Those* is the human antecedent of *who; memories* is the nonhuman antecedent of *which.*]

That can refer to both humans and nonhumans, and some good writers will use *that* interchangeably for *who* or *which.* However, it helps to use *that* when the clause it introduces establishes the identity of the antecedent and to use *who* or *which* when the antecedent already has its identity fairly well established.

> A *man that* drinks and drives *a car that* has faulty brakes does not think much of *his wife who* must sit at home listening to the sounds of night traffic. [*Man* and *car* need identifying. The female human antecedent is already identified by the words *his* and *wife.*]

15 Faulty Pronoun Reference

Pronouns lack specific meaning and must have antecedents to give them this meaning. Like dangling modifiers, pronouns can cause confusion if it is not clear to what they are referring. The correction of faulty pronoun reference depends on what kind of fault is involved.

15A Faulty Pronoun Reference Because of the Omission of the Antecedent

When the antecedent of a pronoun is omitted, the faulty reference can be corrected by putting the antecedent back into its sentence; by substituting the antecedent for the pronoun; or by rewriting the sentence or sentences.

IMPLIED REFERENCE   Instead of setting a total fee, the orthodontist charged twenty dollars a month until the work was completed, *which* the dental profession considers unethical.

CLEAR   Instead of setting a total fee, the orthodontist charged twenty dollars a month until the work was completed, *an arrangement which* the dental profession considers unethical. [antecedent *an arrangement* stated explicitly]

IMPLIED REFERENCE   My father wants me to be a doctor, but *this* is a profession that does not appeal to me.

CLEAR   My father wants me to be a doctor, but *medicine* is a profession that does not appeal to me. [antecedent *medicine* replacing its pronoun]

IMPLIED REFERENCE   I have visited Benson College, but I do not want to go there because *they* are snobs.

CLEAR   On my visit to Benson College, I soon found out that the students are snobs. That's why I do not want to go there. [rewrite]

15B   Faulty Pronoun Reference Because of Reference to More than One Possible Antecedent

When a pronoun refers to more than one antecedent, the reference is ambiguous. The ambiguous reference can be corrected by placing the pronoun close to its antecedent or by rewriting the sentence or sentences.

AMBIGUOUS *Everybody* could see that he was a beautiful little *boy* who looked close-ly.

CLEAR *Everybody who* looked closely could see that he was a beautiful little boy. [pronoun placed close to its antecedent]

CLEAR An observant person could see that he was a beautiful little boy. [rewrite]

AMBIGUOUS *The doctor* told *him* that *he* ought to take a vacation.

CLEAR The doctor said to him, "I really ought to take a vacation." [rewrite]

CLEAR The doctor told him that he had prescribed for himself a long vacation. [rewrite]

15C Faulty Pronoun Reference Because of Undue Separation of Antecedent and Pronoun

If a pronoun is too widely separated from its antecedent, the reference of the pronoun may be obscured. This kind of obscurity can be corrected by substituting the antecedent for the pronoun.

OBSCURE While bathing in the *surf* at Malibu Beach, he was knocked down and almost drowned. *It* was too strong for him.

CLEAR While bathing in *the surf* at Malibu Beach, he was knocked down and almost drowned. *The surf* was too strong for him.

OBSCURE	When *the antecedent* of a pronoun is omitted, the faulty reference can be corrected by putting *it* back into its sentence.
CLEAR	When *the antecedent* of a pronoun is omitted, the faulty reference can be corrected by putting *the antecedent* back into its sentence.

15D Faulty Pronoun Reference Because of Anticipatory Reference

Anticipatory reference is a word order situation where the pronoun in a dependent clause comes before its antecedent in the independent clause. If the sentence is short, the result is acceptable: *When I received it, the shirt was stained.* In longer sentences, however, the reader may be kept uninformed too long about the meaning of the pronoun.

OBSCURE	If *they* are washed gently with warm water and a mild detergent and are then wrapped in a soft, absorbent cloth and left to dry, *these orlon garments* will retain their original shape and texture.
CLEAR	If *these orlon garments* are washed . . . , *they* will retain. . . .

15E Faulty Pronoun Reference Because of Errors of Agreement

An antecedent's control of the form of its pronoun is a strong connecting device inside and outside the sentence. If errors of agreement occur, the connection between the antecedent and its pronoun is blurred. The reader knows what is meant, but his sense of form is offended. The errors of agreement should be corrected (see Section 14), or the usual solutions of rewriting or substituting the antecedent for the pronoun should be employed.

BLURRED

You must keep your *silverware* out of the salty air; *they* will tarnish if you don't.

CLEAR

You must keep your *silverware* out of the salty air; *it* will tarnish if you don't. [*Silverware* is a singular collective noun.]

BLURRED

We were stunned by the riches of *Florence*. *They* have too many museums, galleries, churches, and palaces to count.

CLEAR

We were stunned by the riches of Florence. There are too many museums, galleries, churches, and palaces to count. [*It has too many museums . . .* is possible here, because *it* can stand for Florence. However, the use of *they* may mean that the writer had not Florence in mind but unspecified Florentines.]

BLURRED

James Joyce's Dubliner's is a collection of short stories about the moral life of Dublin. *He* was a native of Dublin and knew intimately the life of the city.

CLEAR

James Joyce's *Dubliner's* is a collection of short stories about the moral life of Dublin. *Joyce* was a native of Dublin and knew intimately the life of the city. [The antecedent *Joyce* is substituted for the pronoun *he*. Strictly speaking, case is not a factor in antecedent-pronoun agreement, but we are offended by the nominative following a possessive case form.]

BLURRED

Students should understand that the college cannot allow registration to be completed unless full payment of fees is made at the time of registration. If paying by check, *you* should make out the check to the bursar of the college.

CLEAR . . . If payment is made by check, the check should be made out to the bursar of the college. [The solution here is to avoid using the pronoun altogether. The passive form of the verb allows for its deletion.]

16 Case

Case denotes the relation of nouns and pronouns to other words in the sentence. There are three relationships or cases:

(1) The nominative case indicates that the noun or pronoun is used as the subject of a verb, or as an appositive to a subject noun, or as a predicate noun.

> *Mary* plays the piano. [nominative case, subject of the verb.]
>
> The younger *girl, Mary,* plays the piano. [*Mary* is in the nominative case as the appositive to *girl.*]
>
> The girl playing the piano is *Mary.* [*Mary* is in the nominative case because it is a predicate noun used after the copulative verb *is* to refer to *girl.*]

(2) The possessive case usually indicates possession.

> I tuned *Mary's* piano.

(3) The objective case indicates that the noun or pronoun receives the action of the verb or the verbal, or that it is the object of a preposition.

> I tuned the *piano.* [object of *tuned*]
>
> Tuning the *piano* was easy. [object of the gerund *tuning*]
>
> She sat down at the *piano* to play. [object of the preposition *at*]

Nouns and pronouns indicate case either by their position in the sentence or by their form. Nouns retain the same form in the nominative and objective cases, but change form to indicate the possessive case: *Mary's.* The personal pronouns, except *you* and *it,* have different forms for the nominative and objective cases as well as for the possessive case. *(I, mine, me; he, his, him; she, hers, her; you, your, yours; it, its.)*

Although speakers need not always strictly adhere to the rules of case, the writer must learn to use nouns and pronouns in their proper case. Nouns cause little trouble because they change form only in the possessive case. The personal pronouns, however, cause some writers considerable difficulty and must therefore be used with special care.

16A Put the Subject of a Verb in the Nominative Case

John is growing taller.

He was born in Vernal, Colorado.

They are studying nuclear physics.

16B Put the Predicate Noun or Pronoun in the Nominative Case

The predicate noun or pronoun stands for the same person or thing as the subject and renames it. Therefore the predicate noun or pronoun is in the same case as the subject, the nominative case.

Mr. Dill is a *sexton.*

It was *he* who wrote the letter.

They thought that the thief was *I.*

16C   Put the Appositive of a Subject in the Nominative Case

Mr. Daly, my *neighbor,* is a probation officer.

The sponsors, *we who are present here,* must sign the petition.

16D   Put the Object of a Verb in the Objective Case

He blew the *whistle.*

We thanked *him* for his kindness.

He taught *her* Greek.

16E   Put the Object or Complement of a Verbal in the Objective Case

Smelling the *coffee,* I jumped out of bed. [*Coffee* is the object of the participle *smelling.*]

Whipping *him does no good.* [*Him* is the object of the gerund *whipping.*]

I should like to be *him.* [*Him* is the predicate complement of the infinitive *to be.*]

16F   Put the Subject of an Infinitive in the Objective Case

We asked *him* to be our representative. [*Him* is the subject of the infinitive *to be.*]

We hired *her* to demonstrate our products. [*Her* is the subject of the infinitive *to demonstrate.*]

16G Put Coordinate Nouns and Pronouns in the Same Case

Mr. Sahn and *I* are on the nominating committee. [*Mr. Sahn* and *I* are subjects of the verb and are therefore in the nominative case.]

He reported *Jones* and *me* to the supervisor. [As objects of *reported, Jones* and *me* are in the objective case.]

16H In All Elliptical Clauses Introduced by *Than* and *As* Put Nouns and Pronouns in the Case Which the Expanded Clause Would Demand

He received the appointment because he has more experience than *I* [*have*].

Mr. Anderson did not recommend him as highly as [he recommended] *me.*

16I Put the Object of a Preposition in the Objective Case

Grandmother's linens will be divided between *you* and *me.* [*You* and *me* are objects of the preposition *between.*]

We will divide the spoils among *us.* [*Us* is the object of the preposition *among.*]

16J Put the Relative Pronoun *Who* or *Whom* in the Case Demanded by Its Use in the Clause to Which It Belongs

Livingston was the man *who* was sent to find Stanley. [*Who* introduces the dependent clause and is in the nominative case because it is the subject of the verb *was sent.*]

Who do you suppose gave him our address? [*Who* is the subject of *gave,* not the object of the parenthetical clause *do you suppose.*]

Whom were they talking about? [*Whom* is the object of the preposition *about.*]

Whom do you take them to be? [*Whom* is the complement of the infinitive *to be.*]

Help *whoever* deserves help. [*Whoever* is the subject of the verb *deserves* and is therefore in the nominative case.]

16K Put Nouns and Pronouns in the Possessive Case When They Are Used to Show the Following

(1) Possession

Carol's store [the store that Carol owns]

his kite

(2) Connection

China's apologists [apologists who represent China

the bureau's legal advisors

(3) The performer of an act

Houdini's escape [Houdini *did* escape.]

the King's abdication

(4) Time, measurement, weight

a day's wages [the wages earned in a day]

a hair's breadth [the width of a hair]

16L   Put a Noun or Pronoun in the Possessive Case When It *Immediately* Precedes a Gerund

Whenever she thinks of *Henry's leaving,* she begins to cry.

I will not take the blame for *somebody's pilfering.*

The dog ran away without *anyone's noticing* him. [Compare this illustration with the next.]

The dog ran away without *anyone* in the house *noticing* him. [Here the possessive case of *anyone* is not used because it does not *immediately* precede the gerund.]

> NOTE: A noun preceding a participle is not in the possessive case.

The *girl painting* in the garden is my sister. [*Painting in the garden* is a participial phrase used as an adjective to modify *girl,* the subject of the verb *is.*]

The *girl's painting* of the garden was given a prize. [*Painting* is a gerund, the subject of the verb *was given.* The possessive case is used because the noun *girl* immediately precedes the gerund *painting.*]

17   Dangling Modifiers

A dangling modifier is a dependent structure which is related to the wrong word in the sentence. It is usually caused by the writer's starting a construction and forgetting where he or she is going. As a result, the sentence is momentarily misleading and often ludicrous.

*Coming around the bend in the road, the church was seen.

In the preceding sentence, the church seems to be coming around the bend, an unusual occupation for an ecclesiastical building. The error is caused by the writer's chopping from the sentence the person who did both the seeing and the coming. The sentence can be repaired by including that person.

> *Coming around the bend in the road,* **he** *saw the church.*

17A Dangling Modifiers Involving Verbals

Most dangling modifiers involve verbals. One way of "undangling" these modifiers is to determine who or what is involved in the action of the verbal and then make sure that this person or thing is in the sentence and that the modifier stands close to it. Another way to correct this error is to transform the verbal back to a finite verb.

(1) *Dangling modifiers will often occur when the structure which the modifer is dependent on has been dropped out of the sentence.*

> **Looking through his field glasses,* the bird flew away.
>
> *Looking through his field glasses,* **he** saw the bird fly away. [Who looked through the field glasses? The bird? More probably **he** did. When **he** is back in the sentence, the participle phrase stands close to it.]
>
> **To bake a delicious cake,* the eggs and butter must be fresh.
>
> *To bake a delicious cake,* **you** must use fresh butter and eggs. [Do eggs and butter bake cakes? No, people generally do that. *One* and **you** are the usual words for people in general. When **you** is placed in the sentence, the infinitive phrase stands close to it.]

(2) *In some instances, the structure that should be modified is in the sentence, but the modifier, by its position, seems to modify something else.*

> **To provide maximum coverage,* you must have a comprehensive **policy.**

To provide maximum coverage, a **policy** must be comprehensive. [The infinitive phrase stands close to **policy.** This infinitive phrase modifier is considered a verb modifier of cause. The original sentence before transformation probably went something like this: *In order that a* **policy** *provide maximum coverage, a* **policy** *must be comprehensive.*]

*The **visitors** watched the construction men at work in the excavation, *gaping in open-mouthed wonder.*

Gaping in open-mouthed wonder, the **visitors** watched the construction men at work in the excavation. [Probably, neither the excavation nor the construction men were gaping in open-mouthed wonder, so the participle phrase stands close to the word it modifies—**visitors.**]

The visitors watched the construction men at work in the excavation *and gaped in open-mouthed wonder.* [The verbal becomes a finite verb to resolve the problem.]

17B Dangling Modifiers Involving Prepositional Phrases and Verbals

Verbals embedded inside prepositional phrases can sometimes relate to the wrong structure. *Before baking a cake, the hands should be washed.* Inside the prepositional phrase which functions as a verb modifier, the verbal is relating to the wrong structure, *the hands.* The methods of correction presented in the previous section also apply here. The prepositional phrase with its verbal is placed close to the nominal involved in the action of the verbal: *Before baking a cake,* **you** *should wash your hands;* or the verbal is transformed into a finite verb so that the prepositional phrase becomes an adverb clause modifying a verb: *Before you bake a cake, you should wash your hands.*

On examining his account, the discrepancy became apparent.

On examining his account, **he** discovered the discrepancy. [*Examining* relates to **he,** while the prepositional phrase *on examining his account* modifies the verb *discovered.*]

When he examined his account, he discovered the discrepancy. [The adverb clause *when he examined his account* modifies the verb *discovered.*]

After beating the eggs, it is time to add the butter.

After beating the eggs, **you** should now add the butter.

After you have beaten the eggs, you should add the butter.

17C   Dangling Modifiers Involving Elliptical Clauses

Elliptical clauses are clauses from which words have been deleted: *when she was eight years old* becomes *when eight years old.* A dangling elliptical clause is one which invites the reader to complete the elliptical clause by putting back the wrong set of words. In the following sentence, the reader is tempted to believe that the father was eight years old. *When eight years old, her father began to teach her Greek.*

The dangling modifier can be corrected by expanding the clause to recover the deleted words. When **she was** *eight years old, her father began to teach her Greek.* Another correction is to leave the elliptical clause as it is but make sure that the nominal *she,* which was deleted, stands close to the clause elsewhere in the sentence. When eight years old, **she** *was taught beginning Greek by her father.*

When thoroughly cleaned, you should wash and salt the fish.

When the **fish has been** *thoroughly cleaned,* it should be washed and salted.

When thoroughly cleaned, the **fish** should be washed and salted.

*While reaching for the salt, his water glass fell over.

While **he was** reaching for the salt, his water glass fell over. [a coincidence on a rocking railroad dining car?]

While reaching for the salt, **he** knocked over his water glass.

17D Generalized Participle Phrases

Some participle phrases have such a wide reference that they do not need a nominal to refer to. We do not care who is speaking in Speaking of taxes, in Sweden taxes have gone up a third in the last four years. In some instances, the participle has lost its sense of action. It is doubtful if anyone is considering in Considering the large amount of advertising, the increase in sales has been disappointing. Certainly, nobody is owing in Owing to certain technical difficulties, the program announced for this time will not be broadcast.

In fact, words and phrases like speaking of, considering, owing to, allowing, granting, assuming, according to, relating to, and concerning function as prepositions and are therefore not regarded as dangling modifiers.

Some of these participles can function as true verbals, and care must be taken to distinguish their two functions.

Granting his weakened condition, he can and must be moved today. [prepositional phrase]

Their leader, granting Caesar's request, allowed him to join their festivities. [participle phrase modifying leader.]

18 Misplaced Modifiers

Because word order in English is very important to the functioning of structures, a modifier which gets out of position can cause confusion. A misplaced modifier usually gets that way because too often we write things down in the order in which they entered our minds. Our minds being what they are, the resulting disorder can produce alarming results. Many a joke has been built around the misplacing of modifiers. *For Sale: 1963 Volkswagen by elderly gentleman recently rebored and new battery installed.* Obviously, it is the Volkswagen and not the elderly gentleman which has been modified by the reboring and battery installation. The solution, then, is to re-order the sentence so that the modifiers clearly modify the right structure.

18A   Misplaced Verb Modifiers

Most verb modifiers can move with some freedom around a sentence. This freedom can too easily become confusion because a verb modifier can attach itself to the wrong verb or noun. The solution is to bring it back close to its verb.

AMBIGUOUS	Jack threatened to divorce her *often.*
CLEAR	Jack *often* threatened to divorce her.
AMBIGUOUS	He offered to paint the fence *last night.* [outdoor late evening painting?]
CLEAR	*Last night* he offered to paint the fence.

18B   Misplaced Noun Modifiers

Noun modifiers have fixed positions before and after the noun. If for any reason, they are dislodged from their correct positions, confusion and ambiguity result. The sentence must be rearranged to get the noun modifier back into its correct position, or the sentence must be recast.

AMBIGUOUS	He finally got rid of his hiccups by holding his breath *which had lasted an hour.*

CLEAR   By holding his breath, he finally got rid of his hiccups *which had lasted an hour.*

CLEAR   He held his breath and stopped his hour-long bout of hiccups.

AMBIGUOUS   He shouted at the bus driver *trembling with rage.* [two angry drivers?]

CLEAR   *Trembling with rage,* he shouted at the bus driver.

Noun modifiers which are prepositional phrases can give particular trouble because if they are misplaced, they not only can refer to other nouns but they also can become verb modifiers on the spot. In the following ambiguous sentence, it is impossible to tell who if anybody is inside that refrigerated show case.

*Ginny showed the rare orchids to the customer *in the refrigerated showcase.*

18C   Double Reference Modifiers

Some structures are so placed that they can refer to the structure before or the structure after them. These squinting modifiers are sometimes completely ambiguous. The use of punctuation to separate the modifier from one of the structures sometimes helps, but it is better to move the squinting modifier to a position where it will look in one direction only.

AMBIGUOUS   The doctor said that if my aunt did not move to a warmer climate *within a year* she would be dead. [Must she move within a year, or will she be dead within a year?]

CLEAR   The doctor said that if my aunt did not move to a warmer climate she would be dead *within a year.*

AMBIGUOUS   While we were dining in Flagstaff, Arizona, *on the advice of a fellow traveler* we decided to see Boulder Dam. [The comma does make the prepositional phrase refer more to Boulder Dam than to dining in Flagstaff, but it is still not clear.]

CLEAR   While we were dining in Flagstaff, Arizona, we decided, *on the advice of a fellow traveler,* to see Boulder Dam.

18D Misplaced Common Adverbs

In colloquial speech, adverbs like *only, almost, merely, scarcely, just,* and *even* are often misplaced without unduly confusing the listener. *Luigi only had $20 with him at the time* is clear in its meaning. In formal writing, however, these adverbs should be placed next to the structures they modify. *Luigi had only $20. . . .*

COLLOQUIAL   He *merely* asked the question because he was curious.

FORMAL   He asked the question *merely* because he was curious.

COLLOQUIAL   She *almost* washed all the dishes. [This sentence is not totally clear; it could mean that she thought about it but watched television instead.]

FORMAL   She washed *almost* all the dishes. [Here she did get her hands wet.]

18E Faulty Phrase Compounding

Faulty phrase compounding is the careless or too enthusiastic compounding of phrases. This kind of compounding involves the placing of several structures to the left of a noun or an adjective. The following is an example of phrase compounding.

A low temperature, steam-operated bronze doughnut press [This machine is probably a bronze press, operated by steam, which stamps out doughnuts at low temperatures. It could also be a press located in a chilly room and stamping out bronze doughnuts.]

Because compounded phrases can be vague or ambiguous and because new compounds are being invented all the time by product packagers, mind-conditioning experts, engineers, and social scientists, great care must be exercised in using these essential but often uncontrollable structures.

Below is a listing of compounded noun and adjective phrases ranging from those long-accepted to those that definitely are to be avoided. Note that the hyphen is used frequently in these compounds. When you are compounding, it is wise to have a good modern dictionary at hand.

(1) *Long-accepted, usable noun-phrase/adjective-phrase compounds*

roadside cafe	The cafe sits beside a road.
waterproof	Something is impervious to water.
baby-sitter	Someone sits with or looks after a baby. [Note that doing the same thing for an old man does not make one an *old man-sitter.]
fly-by-night operation	The operation has a temporary, unreliable character. [To avoid one's creditors, one would leave town in the middle of the night.]

(2) *Acceptable, recently coined noun-phrase/adjective-phrase compounds*

dropout	Someone has dropped out of school or out of organized society.

hang-up	Something has irritated or inhibited someone so that he has become tense. [as if someone had hung him on a hook?]
war-related	Something is related to an activity connected with war-making.
fully automated, disc-oriented computer system	A system of machines that can compute automatically is oriented to a (magnetic) disc.

19 Split Constructions

Because word order is so vital to English, the words of a particular structure should stand together. For emphasis or clarity, a good writer will alter the expected flow of words and structures. However, the pointless separation of words within a structure or of closely related structures may cause awkwardness or obscurity. When separation produces either of these effects, the writer should change the order of the words or revise the sentence.

19A Pointless Separation of Words Within a Structure

The basic elements of a structure such as preposition and object or auxiliary verb and main verb can at times be separated by short intruders like *at times,* but the integrity of the structure is threatened by larger interruptions.

(1) *The verb phrase*

ACCEPTABLE   You *can* never *go* home.

AWKWARD   There stands the house that I *will,* within five years, *purchase and remodel.*

IMPROVED   There stands the house that I will *purchase and remodel* within five years.

(2) *The noun phrase*

AWKWARD   She's *a talented,* and here I must point out that I have good qualifications to make such a judgment, *intelligent person.*

IMPROVED SOMEWHAT   She is a talented person, and because I think that my qualifications are good enough to make such a judgment, I would add further that she is also an intelligent person.

(3) *The infinitive with* to

AWKWARD   I hope that you will be able *to* satisfactorily *repair* my television set within a week.

IMPROVED   I hope that you will be able *to repair* my television set satisfactorily within a week.

AWKWARD   You must begin *to,* if you have the time, *read* more widely in the literature of psychology.

IMPROVED   If you have the time, you must begin *to read* more widely in the literature of psychology.

(4) *The prepositional phrase*

AWKWARD   He pawed through every garment on the bargain counter, looking *for,* in that welter, *a short-sleeved shirt.*

IMPROVED   He pawed through every garment on the bargain counter, looking *for a short-sleeved shirt* in that welter.

19B   Pointless Separation of Closely Related Structures

Closely related structures such as subject, verb, and verb completion, and antecedent and pronoun depend on word order and proximity to signal their relationships. They can be separated by some structures, but larger interruptions strain the fabric of the sentence.

(1) *Basic sentence elements: subject, verb, verb completion*

ACCEPTABLE   *Mean Joe Green,* with savage intensity, *cut down* the opposing quarterback.

AWKWARD   *Mean Joe Green,* and you'll agree when I say his name that he's one of the greatest linemen ever, *played* a great game against Dallas.

IMPROVED   *Mean Joe Green,* one of the greatest linemen to play football, *played* a great game against Dallas. [This illustration cheats a little because the large structure separating the subject from its verb is an appositive, which technically belongs to the noun phrase dependent on *Mean Joe Green.*

AWKWARD   Looking through his binoculars, he *saw* on the opposite shore *a group of bathers.*

IMPROVED   Looking through his binoculars, he *saw a group of bathers* on the opposite shore.

(2) *Coordinated elements*

AWKWARD   *The men removed their hats* when the queen appeared on the balcony *and the ladies cheered.*

IMPROVED   *The men removed their hats and the*

> *ladies cheered* when the queen appeared on the balcony.

(3) *Antecedent and pronoun*

ACCEPTABLE
> *The cows* in the west pasture, *which* were lowing piteously, needed milking. [This separation is justified because in the fixed word order of noun phrases, the prepositional phrase must precede the adjective clause.]

AWKWARD
> He was most impressed by the *applicant,* as I fully expected, *whom* his brother-in-law recommended.

IMPROVED
> As I fully expected, he was most impressed by *the applicant whom* his brother-in-law recommended.

19C Mixed Constructions

In speaking, we sometimes start one structure, slide to another structure, forget the first structure and start all over again. A written court transcript of testimony given under some pressure makes the point well.

> When I got to the door, and just as I was going down the steps, it was about seven thirty I think, well maybe seven thirty-five, I don't tell time too well, anyway I was going to get my car fixed and I saw this man coming up to me, he was about my height and he asked me where Seventh Street was, I think he was wearing a rain. . . .

The initial adverb clauses have long been forgotten as the witness, groping for continuity, continues to mix up his constructions.

In writing, where we usually have the chance to rewrite, the mixed constructions should be tracked down and eliminated.

MIXED

There is no one *to* whom he can apply *to* for help. [Here *to whom* and *whom . . . to* have been blended. The solution is to omit one *to*.]

MIXED

I told him to invest in mutual funds if *he can*. [The direct statement present tense *can* has been left in a sentence transformed to indirect statement. The solutions are to undo or to complete the transform.]

IMPROVED

I told him, "Invest in mutual funds if *you can*."

IMPROVED

I told him to invest in mutual funds if *he could*.

MIXED

In order to complete the installation before the end of the month is why we are working overtime. [The writer] started with an infinitive phrase verb modifier, forgot this fact, and converted it to a nominal subject.]

IMPROVED

In order to complete the installation before the end of the month, we are working overtime. [This is the sentence as first planned. The infinitive phrase is an introductory verb modifier, and the logical subject is *we*.]

IMPROVED

To complete the installation before the end of the month is the reason why we are working overtime. [The writer stays with the conversion of the infinitive phrase to a nominal and makes it the subject of *is*. A final improvement would be to switch the two nominals around so that the sentence started with the noun nominal, *the reason*.]

MIXED | The company repudiated the agreement *which,* although it made several concessions to the union, the terms seemed to be to its advantage. [Before one construction is completed the sentence shifts to another, leaving *which* without a finite verb.]

IMPROVED | The company repudiated the agreement *which,* although it made several concessions to the union, seemed to be to its disadvantage. [*Which* is now the subject of *seemed.*]

MIXED | Agencies must figure out how many people *will* the advertisement *reach.* [This is a transform where the question has not been completely embedded into the declarative sentence. The solutions are to undo the transform by returning to the direct question or to complete the transform by changing the form of the verb to *will reach.*]

IMPROVED | Agencies must ask themselves the following question: how many people *will* the advertisement *reach?*

IMPROVED | Agencies must figure out how many people the advertisement *will reach.*

20 Faulty Comparison

Mistakes are made in writing comparisons because the meanings of the comparative and superlative forms of the adjective pose problems and because elements of a comparison may be wrongly omitted.

20A Faulty Omission of Elements from the Second Part of the Comparison

A comparison is nearly always shortened by the deletion of repeated elements. *She is more beautiful than* her sister (*is*) (*beautiful*). Sometimes the omission of elements from the second half of a comparison can be done badly so that the reader is confused by the ambiguity involved.

The ambiguous sentence *Shaw liked Wagner better than Verdi* has been cut back so that the reader cannot tell whether the original comparison involved Verdi and Shaw as appreciators of Wagner or whether it involved Shaw's appreciation of Wagner and Verdi: *Shaw liked Wagner better than Verdi (liked) (Wagner)* or **Shaw liked Wagner better than (Shaw) (liked) Verdi*. Here is a second example of this kind of deletion problem.

COMPLETE COMPARISON	*Carla ranks Cole Porter higher than Carla ranks Barry Manilow.
FAULTY OMISSION	Carla ranks Cole Porter higher than Barry Manilow. [Manilow has become an evaluator of Cole Porter.]
COMPARISON RESTORED	Carla ranks Cole Porter higher than she ranks Barry Manilow.

20B Omission of the Basis of Comparison

Comparisons should not be approximate. Things being compared should be stated precisely. In the following examples, fuzzy comparisons are made between states and mountains and between filters and cigarettes.

> *The mountains in Vermont are lower and greener than New Hampshire.

> The mountains in Vermont are lower and greener than the *mountains* in New Hampshire. [Mountains are now correctly compared to mountains.]

*The filter in Superbas removes more tars and nicotine than any other cigarette.

The filter in Superbas removes more tars and nicotine than the *filter* of any other cigarette. [Filter is now correctly compared to filter.]

20C Omission of *As* in Double Comparisons

Both *as* and *than* are involved where a comparison is made twice.

In the ring, Tag Martin is as ferocious *as,* if not more ferocious *than,* Jack Dempsey was.

Because the structure looks formidable, a writer will often omit the first comparison word *as.*

*In the ring, Tag Martin is as ferocious, if not more ferocious *than* Jack Dempsey was.

The easiest correction is to avoid the structure altogether and write something with roughly the same meaning. *In the ring, Tag Martin is at least as ferocious as Jack Dempsey.* If the double comparison seems essential, the solution is to separate the two comparisons and delete the second comparison word *than.*

In the ring, Tag Martin is as ferocious *as* Jack Dempsey, if not more ferocious.

20D Confusion of the Normal Meanings of the Comparative and Superlative Forms

The rule is that the comparative form refers to two things; the superlative form refers to more than two things. In speech and colloquial writing, however, the superlative sometimes does the job of the comparative form: *She was certainly the tallest of the twins.* In formal writing, the distinctions between the two forms must be kept. *She is the taller of the twins. I am the oldest of three brothers* (not **I am the older of three brothers*).

20E Confusion of the Meanings of Comparative and Superlative Forms by Misuse of the Word *Other*

The meaning of the comparative form of the adjective, where an individual is *singled out* to be compared to other members of its group, is made explicit by the use of the word **other.** If this word is omitted the result can be confusing.

CONFUSING   Alaska is bigger than any state in the union. [This comparison implies that Alaska is *not* a state in the union.]

CLEAR   Alaska is bigger than any **other** state in the union.

CONFUSING   Charlie is older than any boy in the class. [Charlie is not a boy?]

CLEAR   Charlie is older than any **other** boy in the class.

The superlative form of the adjective is used when an individual is *included* within the members of the group which are being compared to the individual. When the individual is included in the group, the excluding word **other** should not be used.

CONFUSING   Charlie is the oldest of all the **other** boys in the class. [*All* includes Charlie; *other* excludes Charlie.]

CLEAR   Charlie is the oldest of all the boys in the class.

21 Omission of Necessary Words

If structures are not unduly separated and each structure is well constructed, writers will frequently delete words when they feel confident that the construction of the parts of a sentence is clear. When an instruction pamphlet has in it the elliptical structure *when assembling the case for the clock,* we know that words like *you are* have been omitted from the adverb clause *when you are assembling the case of the clock.*

We are expected to fill in the gaps and we do (fill in the gaps). In *He had been tried and judged already,* we supply the *had been* for the second verb. Even when the verb form is not repeated, we can be trusted to think of the right verb form. In the sentence *His manner was offensive, his reasons lame,* the deleted verb form is not *was* but *were.* Some people do object to the lack of repetition because it offends their sense of form, but the meaning is clear.

Because the deletion of words can cause awkwardness and misunderstanding, care must be taken in handling these deletions. There are times when our sense of form is offended; there are times when we have to work to fill in the gaps. Below are listed some of many situations where it is wise not to delete words from their structures.

21A Omission of Necessary Determiners in Coordinate Forms

AMBIGUOUS   When he appeared for the hearing he was accompanied by a friend and advisor. [one or two people?]

CLEAR   When he appeared for the hearing he was accompanied by a friend and *an* advisor. [two people]

CLEAR   When he appeared for the hearing he was accompanied by Jack Lipsky, a friend and advisor. [one person]

AMBIGUOUS   From his income tax he deducted the expenses for his office and show-room. [two places or one place?]

CLEAR   From his income tax he deducted the expenses for his office and *his* showroom. [two places]

21B Omission of Necessary Prepositions

COMPLETE   From his income tax he deducted the expenses for his office and *for* his showroom. [Our sense of form approves the parallelism.]

INCOMPLETE   He has never expressed trust or loyalty to anyone.

COMPLETE   He has never expressed trust *in* or loyalty to anyone. [It is clear what is meant without the preposition *in*. However, we habitually associate certain prepositions with certain nouns and adjectives. Thus our sense of form is pleased by the contrast of *in* and *to*.]

INCOMPLETE   It is either similar or different from each of the preceding propositions.

COMPLETE   It is either similar *to* or different from each of the preceding propositions.

21C Omission of Repeated Verb Forms in Coordinate but Not Parallel Verb Phrases

INCOMPLETE   He had laughed and been reprimanded for his action.

COMPLETE — He had laughed and *had* been reprimanded for his action.

INCOMPLETE — He was late for work and reprimanded by the supervisor.

COMPLETE — He was late for work and *was* reprimanded by the supervisor.

21D Omission of Relationship Words and Other Small Words

TELEGRAPHIC — Reported late to work this morning because of minor accident. Slightly stunned by chilly reception from outer office, warmed by inner sanctum's ho hum attitude.

IMPROVED — *I* reported late to work this morning because of *a* minor accident. *I was* slightly stunned by *the* chilly reception from *the* outer office; *however, I was* warmed by *the* inner sanctum's ho hum attitude.

The telegraphic style should be kept for private papers such as letters, diaries, class notes and telegrams.

Emphasis, Consistency, and Appropriateness

22 Emphasis

It is frequently desirable to emphasize an entire sentence, or a single word or a group of words within a sentence. Without the use of emphasis, writing is flat and uninteresting.

22A Emphasis by Arrangement

To give prominence to an entire sentence, place it at either the beginning or end of the paragraph. The beginning of a paragraph calls attention to itself simply because it is the first thing to engage the reader's attention. The end of a paragraph can be made prominent by building the previous sentences to a climax, or by arranging them in an order of ascending importance so that the thought expressed by the concluding sentence is given added forcefulness by what precedes it.

> The roads were hot and dusty. The grass in the meadows was burned to a parched golden brown. Cattle

in dried-up river bottoms licked hopefully at gravel and rocks where water had always been before. *It had not rained for weeks, and there would be no rain for two more weeks to come.*

To give emphasis to single words or groups of words, pay attention to the arrangement of the order of the words as they occur in the sentence. Words at the beginning and end of a sentence are likely to attract more attention than words in the middle. Words or phrases placed out of their usual or expected positions also call attention to themselves. Careful use of these general principles—avoiding the abuse of straining too hard or too frequently for special effects—is a large part of the secret of varied and effective writing.

In normal English word order, for example, adjectives precede the nouns they modify. Reversing this order calls particular attention to the adjectives.

NORMAL   The *tired old* judge slumped on the bench.

REVERSED   The judge, *old* and *tired*, slumped on the bench.

This procedure cannot be used for a single adjective without producing an overly artificial effect: *The judge, old, slumped on the bench.*

In normal word order the flow of a sentence moves from the subject to the verb and concludes with words related to the verb (as verb completions or modifiers).

The captain led his men into battle. [object *men* and modifier *into battle*]

The young man walked *rapidly down the street because he was anxious to get home.* [adverbial modifers after verb]

The only exception occurs when the sentence is introduced by the expletive *it* or *there: There were forty men in the room.*

The following sentence represents the usual flow of words:

John and Barbara were married on a sunny afternoon in
late November.

[subject]   [verb]   [adverbial modifiers]

The statement is clear, but no part of it is emphasized because the
order of the words is exactly what the reader expects. To give
prominence to adverbial modifiers, place them at the beginning
of the sentence. To emphasize the date, recast the sentence to
read:

In late November, John and Barbara were married on a
sunny afternoon.

To emphasize both the weather and the date, revise the
sentence to read:

On a sunny afternoon in late November, John and
Barbara were married.

Observe particularly how placing the adverbial modifiers (*on a
sunny afternoon in late November*) at the beginning of the
sentence not only makes them more prominent but also gives
greater emphasis to the concluding verb *were married*. Notice,
too, how the abnormal word order of this sentence calls attention
to the entire sentence and makes it more interesting and
emphatic.

The same principle applies to the position of single words in
the sentence.

NORMAL   He drew himself to attention smartly.

EMPHATIC   Smartly he drew himself to attention

To give emphasis to the object of a verb (which normally follows
the verb), place the object at the beginning of the sentence.

NORMAL   They made him president.

EMPHATIC   Him they made president.

In some sentences, a telling and dramatic effect can be achieved
by completely reversing normal word order.

NORMAL   The men marched into the battle.

REVERSED   Into the battle marched the men.

CAUTION: Do not try to recast every sentence, or even the majority of sentences, to secure emphasis. Such a procedure defeats its own purpose by producing an effect of strained and artificial writing. In the following paragraph, the plight of three boys is described. The writer was principally interested in one of the boys, John. He therefore reserves the description of John's misfortune for the end, and he uses abnormal word order only in the concluding sentence.

> They tied Fred to a tree. They perched Jimmy on top of a high rock. John they threw into the river.

Observe how the beginning and end of a sentence call attention to themselves, particularly when the word order is at all unusual. It follows that, even in the construction of ordinary sentences, it is foolish to place unimportant words or phrases in emphatic positions. In the sentence,

> However, the nurse did not arrive.

the sentence modifier *however* does not deserve the emphasis its position gives it. Revising the sentence to

> The nurse, however, did not arrive.

gives prominence to the essential parts of the statement.

Similarly, unimportant words or phrases at the end of a sentence occupy a position of prominence which would be better held by more important material.

> Thousands of spectators packed the stadium to watch the championship game on Thanksgiving Day.

Unless the date is important in this sentence, it should be inserted within the sentence:

> Thousands of spectators packed the stadium on Thanksgiving Day to watch the championship game.

22B Emphasis by Repetition

When a word or phrase is repeated immediately or soon after its original use, the reader is certain to notice the repetition. Deliberate repetition, therefore, is a certain method for obtaining emphasis.

> His father was *weak*, his sister was *weak*, and he was *weak*.

> . . . that government of the *people*, by the *people*, for the *people* . . .

> "Houses of refuge *don't have crews*," said the correspondent. "As I understand them, they are only places where clothes and grub are stored for the benefit of shipwrecked people. They *don't carry crews*."
> "Oh, yes, they do," said the cook.
> "No, they don't," said the correspondent.
> "Well, *we're not there yet*, anyhow," *said the oiler in the stern.*
> "Well," said the cook, "perhaps it's not a house of refuge that I'm thinking of as being near Mosquito Inlet Light. Perhaps it's a life-saving station."
> *"We're not there yet," said the oiler in the stern.*

> — Stephen Crane, "The Open Boat"

22C Emphasis by Use of Voice

The choice of active or passive voice (see section 3E) should depend on which element of the sentence is to be emphasized. In a typical sentence containing a transitive verb, such as

> John owns a horse.

the use of the active voice emphasizes John's ownership. If the statement is intended to answer a question about the horse, it should be placed in the passive voice:

> The horse is owned by John.

In general, if there is no particular problem of emphasis, the active voice is preferable since it is more direct and gives a stronger effect.

> The members will be notified by the president.

is less emphatic than

> The president will notify the members.

22D   Emphasis by Subordination

To give a flat and lifeless effect to writing, the simplest device is to use only simple and compound sentences in normal word order. Writers often do this deliberately to create a pallid atmosphere:

> He went into the house. He looked around listlessly for a few minutes and then slumped into a chair. No sound was heard except the ticking of the clock. He rested his head on the back of the chair and gradually fell into a deep and profound sleep.

But to indicate distinctions between ideas of greater and lesser importance, place the lesser words and phrases in subordinate positions in the sentence (as described in section 22A) and the less important clauses in the subordinate form. In the following sentence, nothing is emphasized, and the entire statement is flat:

> New York City is on the East Coast, and it is America's largest seaport.

To stress the location of New York City, recast the sentence as follows:

> New York City, which is America's largest seaport, is on the East Coast.

To stress the importance of New York City as a seaport, rewrite the sentence:

> New York City, which is on the East Coast, is America's largest seaport.

22E Coordination and Balance

Words and phrases are coordinated by using the coordinating conjunctions *and, but, or, nor, for, yet.*

He was poor *but* happy.

The decor of the lobby was rich, *yet* unobtrusive.

Clauses are coordinated by joining them with a coordinating conjunction or a semicolon.

Ideas of equal importance are given equal prominence by coordination. The elements to be coordinated are given increased emphasis if they are balanced: presented in approximately the same number of words, the same kind of words, and in identical or closely similar word order.

He gained great wealth, but he lost his honor.

To err is human; to forgive, divine.

The man was the hunter; the woman was the cook.

She'll come willingly, or she won't come at all.

Balance also gives effectiveness to simple assertions:

Sauce for the goose is sauce for the gander.

Over the fence is out of bounds.

22F Parallelism and Balance

Two or more ideas which are similar in nature are known as parallel ideas. For effective presentation, express them in parallel form: a noun should be paralleled with a noun, an infinitive with an infinitive, a subordinate clause with another subordinate clause, etc.

PARALLEL NOUNS	They studied *history*, *mathematics*, and *chemistry*.
NOT PARALLEL	They studied about the past, mathematics, and how matter is constituted.

PARALLEL INFINITIVES	He learned *to swim, to play* tennis, and *to ride* a horse.
NOT PARALLEL	He learned to play tennis, swimming, and the art of horseback riding.
PARALLEL CLAUSES	In her praises of the summer camp, she mentioned *that the food was good, that the climate was perfect,* and *that the equipment was superb.*
NOT PARALLEL	In her praises of the summer camp, she mentioned the good food, that the climate was perfect, and what superb equipment they had.
PARALLEL PARTICIPLES	The old house was *battered* by the rain and *bleached* by the sun.
NOT PARALLEL	The old house was battered by the rain and there was no color left because it was standing in the open sunlight.

If possible, balance parallel ideas by expressing them in approximately the same number of words, the same kind of words, and in identical or closely similar word order.

NEITHER PARALLEL NOR BALANCED	He was a good merchant, but was very poor at keeping books.
PARALLEL AND BALANCED	He was a *good merchant,* but a *poor bookkeeper.*
NEITHER PARALLEL NOR BALANCED	He believed in democracy for the upper classes, but felt that the common people should be ruled by their superiors.

PARALLEL AND
BALANCED

He believed in *democracy for the classes*, but *autocracy for the masses*.

PARALLEL AND
BALANCED

It is wiser *to invest than to squander, to seek out friends than to collect acquaintances, to treasure life than to throw it away*.

Notice how parallelism, balance, and repetition are combined in the following celebrated pasage from I Corinthians 13:

Though I speak with the tongues of men and of angels, and have not charity, I am become as sounding brass, or a tinkling cymbal. And though I have the gift of prophecy, and understand all mysteries, and all knowledge; and though I have all faith, so that I could remove mountains, and have not charity, I am nothing. And though I bestow all my goods to feed the poor, and though I give my body to be burned, and have not charity, it profiteth me nothing.

Charity suffereth long, and is kind; charity envieth not; charity vaunteth not itself, is not puffed up, doth not behave itself unseemly, seeketh not her own, is not easily provoked, thinketh no evil; rejoiceth not in iniquity, but rejoiceth in the truth; beareth all things, believeth all things, hopeth all things, endureth all things.

Charity never faileth: but whether there be prophecies, they shall fail; whether there be tongues, they shall cease; whether there be knowledge, it shall vanish away. For we know in part, and we prophesy in part. But when that which is perfect is come, then that which is in part shall be done away.

When I was a child, I spake as a child, I understood as a child, I thought as a child: but when I became a man, I put away childish things. For now we see through a glass, darkly; but then face to face; now I know in part; but then shall I know even as also I am known. And now abideth faith, hope, charity, these three; but the greatest of these is charity.

23   Consistency

In dealing with any subject, decide in advance on the method of treating the subject. Then endeavor to be consistent, avoiding such departures from the selected method as might creep in through carelessness or forgetfulness.

23A   Consistency in Tense

When writing a narrative, decide on a basic tense and do not change it unless the reference to some prior or subsequent event demands a change.

INCONSISTENT   John *sprang* to his feet when he *heard* the whistle. He *ran* as fast as he could to reach the upper deck. There he *sees* a battleship bearing down on them. [Inconsistent change to present tense] He *would remember that moment for years to come. [Consistent because the reference is to the future]*

23B   Consistency in Number

When discussing a type or a class, decide in advance whether to use the singular or plural number and do not change it.

INCONSISTENT   The automatic washing *machine* is a great invention. *It* saves *homemakers* many hours of drudgery. *These machines* are among the most wonderful inventions of the twentieth century.

CONSISTENT   The automatic washing *machine* is a great *invention*. *It* saves the *homemaker* many hours of drudgery. *This machine* is *one* of the most wonderful inventions of the twentieth century.

23C Consistency in Person

Decide in advance whether a piece of writing is to be personal or impersonal, and do not change the point of view.

> INCONSISTENT When learning to play a piano, *the student* should remember that great care and precision are essential. *You* should practice simple pieces until they are completely mastered. *One* can never succeed in an art if the fundamentals are neglected.

In this paragraph, either the *You* in the second sentence should be changed to *He or she* or the entire paragraph should be written as a direct appeal to the reader, as:

> When learning to play a piano, remember that great care and precision are essential. You should practice simple pieces until they are completely mastered. You can never succeed in an art if you neglect the fundamentals.

23D Consistency and Appropriateness in Tone

Unless you wish to jar the reader by some sudden intrusion, keep the tone and level of writing constant. Informal or chatty writing admits the use of slang or colloquialisms which are out of keeping with formal writing. The appropriateness of words in given contexts is learned only by reading and listening. But notice the absurdity of the following:

> The dean exhorted the statutory members of the faculty to redouble their efforts and *get going*.

> I get sick and tired of hearing you squawk about your *lassitude*.

> Fourscore and seven years ago, our fathers brought forth on this continent a new nation, conceived in Liberty, and dedicated to the proposition that *highbrows are no better than lowbrows*.

There are many synonyms in the English language which, although nearly identical in meaning, are appropriately used only in certain connections. The word *love* means *zero*, but only in the game of tennis. *Tip, gratuity*, and *perquisite* all mean some kind of value received as incidental and variable rather than as fixed income. In normal usage, however, the word *tip* is connected with frequent small amounts of money for trivial services, *gratuity* with a considerable sum of money in reward for lengthy service, and *perquisite* with certain emoluments or values which accompany political offices and some professions. Similarly, *salary, pay, wage, fee*, and *honorarium* are roughly synonymous, but are applicable to different types and levels of monetary remuneration. When taking a position, a lawyer is *retained*, a laborer is *hired*, a minister is *called*, a clerk is *employed*, a physician is *consulted*.

Be observant of word usage in your reading. When consulting a dictionary, read the entire entry, not just one of the definitions, to get as much of a sense of the word as possible.

24 Variety

The type of sentence structure appropriate to a given piece of writing depends on the nature of the subject, the purpose of the author, and the anticipated audience. Directions, for example, should be written in simple language and short sentences.

To reach the Denby Road Church:

1. Follow Route 4 to Carmine Street.

2. Turn right and continue to the second traffic signal (Denby Road).

3. Turn left on Denby Road.

4. You will see the church on the righthand side of the street.

Short, direct sentences are also effective in describing action:

A succession of loud and shrill screams, bursting suddenly from the throat of the chained form, seemed to thrust me violently back. For a brief moment I hesitated—I trembled. Unsheathing my rapier, I began to grope with it about the recess; but the thought of an instant reassured me. I placed my hand upon the solid fabric of the catacombs, and felt satisfied. I reapproached the wall. I replied to the yells of him who clamored. I reechoed—I aided—I surpassed them in volume and in strength. I did this, and the clamorer grew still.

— Edgar Allan Poe, "The Cask of Amontillado"

In other kinds of writing where no special effect is sought for, avoid monotony by varying the lengths of sentences and by avoiding a series of sentences with nearly identical structure and word order, such as occur in the following example:

When I was a boy, my comrades and I had only one permanent ambition: to be steamboatmen. Although we had transient ambitions of other sorts, they were only transient. When a circus came and went, it left us all burning to become clowns. When the first negro minstrel show came to town, we all wanted to try that kind of life. Every once in a while, we all had the ambition to become pirates. Although all of these ambitions gradually faded out, the ambition to be steamboatmen always remained.

Essentially the same material is given variety and interest by sentences of varied length and structure in Mark Twain's *Life on the Mississippi*:

When I was a boy, there was but one permanent ambition among my comrades in our village on the west bank of the Mississippi River. That was, to be a steamboatman. We had transient ambitions of other sorts, but they were only transient. When a circus came and went, it left us all burning to become clowns; the first negro minstrel show that ever came to our section left us all suffering to try that kind of life; now and then we had a hope that, if we lived and were good, God would permit us to be pirates. These ambitions faded out, each in its turn; but the ambition to be a steamboatman always remained.

In the following selection, the opening of William Hazlitt's essay *On Familiar Style*, notice how the first short, direct sentence attracts attention. Then notice the varied length of the second, third, and fourth sentences which are followed by an effective parallelism in the fifth sentence. The sixth sentence, quite long, acts as a kind of summation.

[1.] It is not easy to write a familiar style. [2.] Many people mistake a familiar for a vulgar style, and suppose that to write without affectation is to write at random. [3.] On the contrary, there is nothing that requires more precision, and, if I may say so, purity of expression, than the style I am speaking of. [4.] It utterly rejects not only all unmeaning pomp, but all low, cant phrases, and loose, unconnected, *slipshod* allusions. [5.] It is not to take the first word that offers, but the best word in common use; it is not to throw words together in any combinations we please, but to follow and avail ourselves of the true idiom of the language. [6.] To write a genuine familiar or truly English style, is to write as any one would speak in common conversation, who had a thorough command and choice of words, or who could discourse with ease, force, and perspicuity, setting aside all pedantic and oratorical flourishes.

Punctuation

Punctuation is a device used to assist the reader. It takes the place of changes in tone, inflection, and volume, and of pauses, facial expressions, etc., by which a speaker makes his meaning clear.

25 Terminal Punctuation

25A The Period

The principal use of the period is to indicate the end of a sentence which is not a question or an exclamation.

The president was elected.	[statement]
I asked if he would see me.	[indirect question]
Please shut the door.	[request or command]

The period is often used for terminal purposes when a sentence is not involved, as after numbers in a list:

1. The President

2. The Council

3. The Board of Trustees

The period is used to terminate most abbreviations:

> e.g., i.e., Mr., Dr., Rev., etc.

Three periods are used to indicate the omission of one or more words or even sentences in a quotation:

> "I pledge allegiance . . . to the republic . . ."

When the omission occurs after the end of a sentence, the three periods are added after the period which terminates the sentence:

> "Shakespeare was born in 1564. . . . He married Anne Hathaway in 1582."

25B   The Question Mark

The question mark is used to terminate a direct question of any sort:

> Who are you? Why? Why not? He did?

When enclosed in parentheses, the question mark indicates uncertainty or doubt:

> He lived from 1635 (?) to 1680.

25C   The Exclamation Point

Use the exclamation point to terminate a strong expression of feeling. Do not use it for indications of mild emotion.

> Nonsense! I don't believe you.

> I'll shoot the first man who moves!

> Get out of this house at once!

Be sparing in the use of exclamations. The effectiveness of exclamation points is dulled by overuse.

26 The Comma

The comma is the most frequently used (and abused) aid to reading. Most poor users of commas annoy their readers by inserting illogical commas or too many commas. There is no need for uncertainty if the basic principles governing the use of the comma are clearly understood.

26A To Separate Parts of a Series

Use the comma to separate words, phrases, or clauses in a series. It is a substitute for a coordinating conjunction.

> John, Fred, Harry, Frank
>
> [John and Fred and Harry and Frank]

Usually the final element in the series is preceded by *and* or *or* to indicate the nature and the termination of the series.

> John, Fred, Harry, and Frank

A comma before the terminating conjunction (*and* or *or*), although not absolutely essential, is used to prevent confusion because of the not infrequent appearance of *and* within the members of a series:

> She shopped at Johnson's, Ward and Nelson's, and French's.
>
> He ate soup, meat and potatoes, and pie.
>
> He went across the sidewalk, down the street, and into the bar and grill.
>
> She asked to see the manager, she complained about the merchandise and the service, and she got satisfaction.

A single adjectival modifying a noun is frequently so necessary that it may be considered a part of the identification: *pine* tree, *drinking* glass, *red* dress. Another adjective preceding such an adjective-noun phrase functions as if it modified the entire phrase and is therefore not separated from the phrase by a comma: *tall* pine tree, *large* drinking glass, *beautiful* red dress.

To call attention to each adjective as individually and separately describing the noun, use a comma to separate the adjectives:

> a tall, dark, distinguished gentleman

A comma between adjectivals has the same effect as the conjunction *and.*

> a tall and dark and distinguished gentleman

26B   To Separate the Clauses of a Compound Sentence Joined by a Coordinating Conjunction

Use the comma to separate the independent clauses of a compound sentence when they are joined by a coordinating conjunction. The comma is placed immediately before the conjunction (*and, but, or, not, for, yet*) to indicate that the conjunction introduces a clause.

> The mayor invited the members of the committee to lunch, *and* most of them accepted her invitation.
>
> I haven't succeeded in balancing my checkbook, *yet* I plan to continue writing checks.

When the clauses are very short so that most or all of the sentence can be taken in instantaneously by the eye, the comma is not required.

> He sent for her and she came.

26C   To Separate Interjections and Similar Nonintegrated Sentence Elements

Occasionally, words or phrases in a sentence are not integrated in the sentence structure. That is, they do not modify specific words, they are not subjects or verbs, they are not objects of prepositions, etc. Separate such nonintegrated words or phrases from the remainder of the sentence by commas.

(1) Use the comma to set off interjections which are included in sentences.

> *Oh*, I thought so.
>
> *Hey,* watch your step!
>
> *Hello*, I'm glad to see you.

If the interjection occurs within the sentence, it is separated by two commas.

> I tried so hard, *alas*, to do it.

Use the comma to set off any other words or phrases which behave as interjections:

> *a.* The adverbs *yes, no* are frequently used as interjections.
>
> > *Yes,* I'll be glad to.
>
> *b.* Terms of direct address are normally used as interjections.
>
> > *John,* get the book.
> >
> > *You over there,* put on your hat.

(2) Use the comma to set off sentence modifiers. Words like *however, moreover, furthermore, therefore, nevertheless* and phrases like *on the other hand, in addition, to the contrary* often modify the whole sentence instead of a single word within the sentence. To make clear that they are not intended to modify a single word, separate them from the rest of the sentence by commas.

> *However,* she caught the train.
>
> He tried, *moreover*, to attain his goal.
>
> *On the other hand*, he wasted his money.

(3) Use the comma to set off absolute phrases. An absolute phrase, made up of a noun or pronoun and a participle (*the sun having risen*), is another kind of sentence modifier. Absolute

phrases are not connected to the remainder of the sentence by relating words such as prepositions or conjunctions. They are therefore set off by commas.

> *The river being cold,* we did not go swimming.

> It seemed sensible, *the weather being warm*, to pack a lunch.

26D To Set Off a Long Phrase or Clause Preceding the Subject

Since the first element in an English sentence is normally its subject, any phrase or clause of five words or more preceding the subject is concluded with a comma to indicate that the subject is about to appear.

> *During the long winter of 1881*, the king suffered a severe illness.

> *When I see robins on the lawn,* I know that spring is here.

> *Having reached the age of discretion,* she was no longer supervised.

If the phrase is so short that the reader can take in both the phrase and the subject in a single eye-fixation, the comma is not necessary.

> *In 1881* the king suffered a severe illness.

26E To Indicate Interruptions of Normal Word Order

Set off by commas: any words, phrases, or clauses which interrupt normal word order. Normally, adjectives precede the nouns they modify, and, normally, subjects are followed by verbs or by modifying phrases or clauses:

> The old and respected firm in the city went bankrupt.

If, for purpose of emphasis, the adjectives *old* and *respected* follow the noun *firm,* they are set off by commas:

The firm, old and respected, went bankrupt.

A single comma should never interrupt the natural flow of a sentence, as from subject to verb or from verb to verb completion. But intruding elements of any kind should be indicated by being preceded and followed by commas.

The river, it seems likely, will overflow its banks.

The year of his graduation, 1950, was an eventful one.

She was a tall and, to put it mildly, buxom woman.

26F To Set Off Nonrestrictive Elements

Any word, phrase, or clause that is not essential to the meaning of a sentence is called nonrestrictive. Set off nonrestrictive elements by commas.

Some words, like *scurrilous*, are difficult to spell.

His father, Mr. Smith, was ill.

The Homeric epics, the *Iliad* and the *Odyssey*, are long poems.

His uncle, who is a doctor, is coming for a visit.

Be careful to distinguish between such nonrestrictive elements and restrictive elements. Restrictive words, phrases, or clauses are necessary to the meaning of a sentence and are never set off by commas.

Shakespeare's play *Hamlet* is a masterpiece. [The name of the play is essential to the meaning.]

Dante's epic, *The Divine Comedy,* is made up of one hundred cantos. [It is Dante's only epic; its name is therefore not essential.]

The people who sat in the balcony paid less for their seats. [The clause *who sat in the balcony* is restrictive.]

My brother, who sat in the balcony, enjoyed the play.

[The location of his seat is not considered essential to the statement being made.]

By insertion or omission of commas, the writer can indicate whether elements are restrictive or not.

His dog Rover is a collie. [The lack of commas indicates that he has several dogs. One of them is named Rover.]

His dog, Rover, is a collie. [He owns only one dog. The name is given but it is not essential.]

When the nonrestrictive element occurs at the end of the sentence, the comma preceding it indicates its relative unimportance.

The president was interviewed by a large group of reporters, who were informally dressed.

26G To Separate Contrasted Sentence Elements

Use the comma to emphasize the contrast between two parts of a sentence.

He wanted to see a psychiatrist, not a lawyer.

His diet was wholesome, not appetizing.

She longed to find happiness, but found misery instead.

26H To Prevent Misreading

Use the comma to prevent misreading when the sequence of words in a sentence might lead to momentary confusion.

During the summer, days become longer.

Without the comma, the reader might well read *summer days* as adjectival-noun.

Soon after, the meeting was adjourned.

Without the comma, the reader might read *after the meeting* as a prepositional phrase, and this fragment would have no subject.

> The lawyer interviewed John and Fred, and seemed very happy about what they had to say.

In this sentence the two *and's* occur in close proximity. The first joins the nouns *John* and *Fred;* the second joins the verbs *interviewed* and *seemed.* The comma after *Fred* clarifies the structure of the sentence.

26I Conventional Uses of the Comma

Certain uses of the comma have become established by convention.

- Following the salutation of an informal letter: *Dear Mildred,*

- Following the complimentary close of a letter: *Yours truly,*

- Separating dates of the month from the year: *June 19, 1942*

- Separating parts of an address: *Mr. John Smith, 138 Elm Street, Syracuse, N.Y. 13082*

- Separating numbered or lettered divisions or subdivisions: *Book III, Chapter 9;* or *III, 9;* or *A, d*

- Separating names from distinguishing titles: *Frank Jones, Jr.* or *Edward French, Ph.D.*

- Separating thousands in large figures: *1,497,341*

- Separating a direct quotation from the indication of the speaker (Section 34B).

- Placed before and after introductory words and abbreviations such as *i.e., e.g.,* and *for example:* Some plays are known as closet dramas; i.e., they were written to be read rather than acted.

27 Misuse of the Comma

Do not annoy the reader by inserting commas where they are not required. Commas are intended to help the reader; unnecessary commas only confuse.

27A Do Not Interrupt the Normal Flow of Thought by a Comma

WRONG   The fact that the train had broken down halfway between its point of departure and its destination, was sufficient reason for the passengers to malign the railroad. [The subject is a long clause, but it is entirely clear. It opens the sentence as expected, and it is followed immediately by the verb. Inserting a comma after *destination* merely impedes the flow of thought.]

WRONG   The carpenter insisted, that he knew what he was doing. [The comma after *insisted* separates the verb from its object.]

WRONG   He drove a hard, sharp, painful, bargain. [The comma after *painful* separates the adjective *painful* from the word it modifies.]

27B Do Not Separate Words or Phrases Joined by *And* or *Or*

WRONG   He went to the office, and opened his mail. [*And* joins the compound verb *went* and *opened*. It does not join two clauses.]

27C Do Not Place a Comma Between a Conjunction and the Word or Words It Introduces

WRONG He was tired but, he refused to stop driving.

WRONG The lonely woman continued to hope that, her son was still alive.

---

28 The Semicolon

The semicolon functions midway between the comma and the period as an indication of a pause. It is stronger than the comma and weaker than the period.

28A To Separate Independent Clauses

The principal use of the semicolon is to mark the dividing point in a compound sentence, the clauses of which are not joined by a coordinating conjunction.

  The policeman stood on the corner; he was watching the traffic pattern at the intersection.

  The boss had a good sense of humor; nevertheless, he was a strict supervisor.

28B To Separate Major Word Groupings from Lesser Ones

A proliferation of commas in a sentence may lead to confusion. The semicolon, as a stronger mark, is therefore useful in punctuating major elements which themselves contain commas.

He visited several colleges, schools, and institutions; several factories, office buildings, and churches; and a number of public buildings of a miscellaneous nature. [The three major divisions, the first two of which contain commas, are clarified by the use of the semicolon.]

The old horse, tired and hungry after its long journey over the long, hilly, rutted country roads, finally staggered and fell; and it was a long time before it could be persuaded to get up again. [The individual clauses of the compound sentence, the first of which contains several commas, are clearly indicated by the semicolon.]

29 The Colon

The colon means *as follows*. It is principally used to introduce a list (frequently in conjunction with such words as *following* or *as follows*). It should not be used to introduce a short list such as *He raised beans, peas, apples, pears, and plums.*

The gentlemen who contributed to the fund were: John Doe, Frank Smith, Eliot Doolittle, Ezra Jones, Samuel Greenbaum, John MacMillan, Edward Stritch, James Hoffman, Nelson Brown.

The principles on which the club was founded are as follows:

1. The establishment of a revolving fund for education.
2. The provision of entertainment for the children.
3. Monthly social meetings for the adults.

Occasionally the colon is used to introduce a single word or phrase to add dramatic significance.

He had only one thing to live for: death.

The colon can be used to introduce a single word, phrase, or clause when it acts as a substitute for the words *as a result.*

The president died: the firm failed.

The colon is used after the salutation of a business letter (*Dear Sir:* or *To Whom It May Concern:*) and to divide subdivisions from major divisions as in recording time (*12:25*) or Biblical references (*Genesis 10:3*).

30 The Dash

The dash is used to indicate a sharp or sudden break in the normal or expected flow of sentence structure. (In typing, a dash is represented by two hyphens.)

He asked me—what was he thinking?—to marry him.

I hoped that he—. But I'd rather not talk about it.

The dash may be used to separate parenthetical ideas or ideas inserted as an afterthought.

PARENTHETICAL   The New York skyline—especially when viewed for the first time—is a breathtaking sight.

AFTERTHOUGHT   He ran down the hill with the speed of an express train—or so it seemed.

The dash is used in dialogue to describe hesitating or halting speech.

"I mean—I think—I think I mean," he began hesitantly. "I think I mean I'd make a good husband."

31 The Hyphen

The hyphen is used to make a compound word out of two or more words which are intended to be read as a single unit.

The Dartmouth-Brown game

Mr. John King-Smith

A high-pressure salesman

A sugar-coated pill

A holier-than-thou expression

The hyphen is used to eliminate ambiguities or misreadings which occasionally result from the addition of a prefix.

re-press   re-fry   re-sign

The hyphen is used to indicate that the remainder of a word is to follow when the word is broken at the end of a line. Words may not be divided arbitrarily; they may be broken only between syllables. (Syllables are the parts of a word which are naturally pronounced as units. When in doubt about correct division into syllables, consult a good dictionary.)

> Samuel Johnson, who was an outstanding literary fig-
> ure of the eighteenth century in England, was known
> as the great lexicographer. He compiled the first
> English dictionary.

The hyphen is used with compound numbers from *twenty-one* to *ninety-nine*.

The hyphen is used to separate dates of birth and death: *John Barton* (1181–1214); scores of games: 13–12; and other figures where the relationship between them is obvious.

32   The Apostrophe

Apart from indicating possession (see Section 1D), the apostrophe is principally used to indicate letters in a contraction.

Who's there? I can't come.

The apostrophe is also used to form plurals of letters, figures, or signs for which there is no acceptable plural.

There are three 9's, twenty-seven n's, and two *'s on the page.

33 Parentheses and Brackets

Parentheses are used to enclose materials which are so intrusive as to be an annoying interruption of sentence structure.

It is important (importance being understood to be a relative matter) to obey the law.

The law was passed (1) to satisfy the governor, (2) to please the people, and (3) to provide greater safety.

The houses were classified as (*a*) bungalows, (*b*) ranch-type houses, (*c*) split-level houses.

His novel *The Homeward Trail* (1917) was a best-seller.

Brackets are used to enclose additions by the editor to any kind of quoted matter.

"The author [Mark Twain] was known primarily as a humorist."

"He was born in 1835 [?] in a small southern town."

34 Quotations and Quotation Marks

34A Quotation Marks to Indicate Titles

Quotations marks are used to indicate titles of short works such as articles in magazines, short stories, one-act plays, essays, short poems, and chapter titles.

"The Raven" [short poem]

"The Murders in the Rue Morgue" [short story]

"Bound East for Cardiff" [one-act play]

34B Direct Quotations

Quoted materials, whether oral or written, are indicated by being enclosed in quotation marks. Only the exact words of the original speaker or writer should be so enclosed. An indirect quotation or a report of the substance of what was said or written should not be enclosed by quotation marks.

DIRECT   He said, "I am going home."

INDIRECT   He said that he was going home.

DIRECT   She said, "I have a headache. I am going to bed."

INDIRECT   She said that her head hurt and that she was going to bed.

DIRECT   The opening words of the chapter are "I continued at home with my wife and children."

INDIRECT   The opening words of the chapter state that the author stayed at home with his wife and children.

COMBINED   She said that she had "no intentions" of staying.

In direct quotations, indications of the speaker (*he said, she asked*) are separated from the quotation by a comma or marked off by two commas if reference to the speaker is placed within a sentence.

"Please don't tell my mother," he whined.

The nurse replied, "That's exactly what I intend to do."

"Well, at least," he entreated, "don't tell her everything."

When the indication of the speaker is placed at the end of a quotation which concludes with a question mark or an exclamation mark, the comma is omitted.

> "Don't you know enough to stop?" he asked.

> "Let me go!" she shrieked.

If the quotation consists of more than one sentence, only one sentence is joined to the indication of the speaker.

> "My son wants to buy this," she said. "How much will it cost?"

> "I wouldn't do that," he remonstrated. "You might get into trouble."

In quotations other than dialogue, the punctuation and capitalization of quoted matter is reproduced exactly as it was originally written.

> The author believes that "Capitalism is here to stay."

> The novel reflected the author's "growing concern with the problem of juvenile delinquency."

If the quotation is longer than one paragraph, no end quotation marks are placed at the conclusion of the first paragraph. All succeeding paragraphs are prefaced by quotation marks, but only the final paragraph is concluded with end quotation marks.

Long quotations (ten lines or more) from writings are not enclosed in quotation marks. They are set off from the original writing by indentation. Smaller typeface is customary for printed matter and single spacing for typewritten material.

34C Quotations Within Quotations

Single quotation marks are used to indicate a quotation within a quotation.

> "I've just read Shelley's 'Ode to the West Wind,' " she said.

The alternation of double and single quotation marks is continued for the inclusion of quotations within quotations within other quotations. Such complexities should be avoided, of course, but the following is an example of the technique:

> "Are you aware," asked the lawyer, "that the defendant precisely stated, 'I did not read "The Bride Said, 'No'" '?"

Be sure that all opening quotation marks are balanced by end quotation marks.

34D Quotation Marks Used with Other Punctuation

The placing of quotation marks in connection with other punctuation follows the standard procedures instituted by printers for the sake of the physical appearance of the page. Periods and commas are always placed inside end quotation marks.

> "I wanted," he said, "to go home."

Colons and semicolons are always placed outside end quotation marks. Other marks are placed where they logically belong—within the quotation if they punctuate the quotation, outside the quotation if they punctuate the sentence of which the quotation is a part.

> He called his friend "old frog"; he didn't mean it as an insult.

> He assimilated the advice given in the pamphlet "How to Study"; he passed the course.

> "How are you?" I asked.

> How can I tell that "Whatever is, is right"?

> Beware of "the valley of the shadow of death"!

34E Punctuation of Dialogue

Standard practice in the punctuation of dialogue calls for a new paragraph for each change of speaker. Descriptive or other materials related to the speaker are contained in the same paragraph as the quotation.

"I knew it!" said the toper to the shepherd with much satisfaction. "When I walked up your garden before coming in, and saw the hives all of a row, I said to myself, 'Where there's bees, there's honey, and where there's honey, there's mead.' But mead of such a truly comfortable sort as this I really didn't expect to meet in my older days." He took yet another pull at the mug, till it assumed an ominous elevation.

"Glad you enjoy it!" said the shepherd, warmly.

"It is a goodish mead," assented Mrs. Fennel, with an absence of enthusiasm which seemed to say that it was possible to buy praise for one's cellar at too heavy a price. "It is trouble enough to make, and really I hardly think we shall make any more. For honey sells well, and we ourselves can make shift with a drop o' small mead and metheglin for common use from the comb-washings."

"Oh, but you'll never have the heart!" reproachfully cried the stranger in cinder-gray, after taking up the mug a third time and setting it down empty.

"I love mead when 'tis old like this, as I love to go to church o' Sundays, or to relieve the needy any day of the week."

"Ha, ha, ha!" said the man in the chimney-corner, who, in spite of the taciturnity induced by the pipe of tobacco, could not or would not refrain from this slight testimony to his comrade's humor.

— Thomas Hardy, "The Three Strangers"

A particular advantage of this convention is that when only two speakers are involved, the alternation of paragraphs makes it unnecessary to identify each speaker in turn and allows the dialogue to be paced more rapidly and without interruptions.

"Everybody believed the story, didn't they?" said the dirty-faced man, refilling his pipe.

"Except Tom's enemies," replied the bagman. "Some of 'em said Tom invented it altogether; and others said he was drunk, and fancied it, and got hold of the wrong trousers by mistake before he went to bed. But nobody ever minded what *they* said."

"Tom said it was all true?"

"Every word."

"And your uncle?"

"Every letter."

"They must have been very nice men, both of 'em," said the dirty-faced man.

"Yes, they were," replied the bagman; "very nice men indeed!"

— Charles Dickens, "The Bagman's Story"

35 Italics

Italics is a term used to designate a particular font of printer's type in which the letters slant upwards to the right as in the word *italics*. In written or typed material, italics are indicated by underlining.

35A Italics to Indicate Titles of Full-Length Works

Use italics to indicate the titles of novels, full-length plays, long book-length poems, full-length motion pictures, and the titles of books in general. They are also used to indicate names of magazines or periodical publications of any sort. This usage in conjunction with quotation marks helps to distinguish the chapter from the complete book, the poem from the collection in which it appears, the article from the magazine, etc.

Hamlet   *A Tale of Two Cities*   *The Atlantic Monthly*

EXCEPTIONS: Through convention, the Bible and the books of the Bible are neither italicized nor put in quotation marks. The place of publication of newspapers (normally regarded as part of the title) is frequently not italicized.

Genesis   *The New York Times*   The Iowa *Gazette*

35B   Italics to Indicate Words or Letters Used as Such

Use italics to indicate words or letters which are used as such, that is, words or letters considered independent of their meaning.

The word *benign* is sometimes misspelled.

The letter *I* should be capitalized when used alone.

35C   Italics for Emphasis

Italics are occasionally used (though very rarely) to give emphasis to a particular word or group of words. This usage should be avoided and resorted to only when no other method of stressing the word is available, as in the reporting of dialogue or in the writing of plays.

"I didn't mean your husband; I meant *you!*"

The Paragraph

Paragraphs are the structural units of composition. An essay or a narrative consists of a group of related paragraphs that develop the thought of the whole. To write logically and effectively, therefore, one must master the principles of paragraphing.

36 The Paragraph Defined

Thoughts are stated in sentences, but they are developed in paragraphs. Whereas a sentence states that May is a lovely month, a paragraph develops the statement by expressing the qualities of sunshine and warmth, of gentle rains, and of blossoming that make May a lovely month. A paragraph, therefore, is a group of related sentences that expand a statement by explaining it, or illustrating it, or proving it. A paragraph gives a statement substance and weight, invests it with meaning, and charges it with conviction. A reader may miss or dismiss a statement, but is held by a paragraph and urged to understand and believe.

Just as a paragraph contains a group of related sentences, an essay or narrative contains a group of related paragraphs. Each paragraph develops a logical unit of thought. Each paragraph is logically related to the paragraph that precedes it and to the paragraph that follows. All of the paragraphs combine to express the design and purpose of the whole. Therefore, paragraphs are, as already stated, the structural units of composition.

A paragraph is also a device of punctuation. The indented first line identifies the paragraph, separates it from the preceding and following paragraphs, and shows where a thought begins and ends. Physically the paragraph breaks what would otherwise be a solid block of writing into small units, thus giving the reader some relief. The reader may pause between paragraphs, mark the progress, and read on with a sense of direction.

Although paragraphs usually contain several sentences, undeveloped paragraphs of one or two sentences are frequently used for the following purposes:

(1) In essays, to summarize what has been said, to guide the reader from section to section, or to emphasize an important point.

(2) In dialogue, to indicate a new speech or a new speaker. A paragraph of dialogue may therefore contain only a phrase or a word:

> "Are you Frank Jones?" he asked.
> "Yes."
> "And you live here?"
> "I do."

(3) In newspapers, to make the layout attractive and to express facts and opinions simply and emphatically.

Normally, however, a paragraph states a topic, develops it, relates it to other paragraphs, and contributes to the design and purpose of the whole essay. In short, a paragraph is, as already stated, a logical unit of composition. Anyone who wishes to write clearly and logically must be able to plan and write paragraphs.

36A   Indent the First Line of Every Paragraph an Inch in Handwritten Manuscripts and Five Spaces in Typescript

> The next morning we arose before dawn. Mother studied the road map, and Father loaded the car. . . .

36B Develop the Paragraph with Material Suitable to the Topic

The kinds of substance and the methods most commonly used to develop paragraphs are the following:

(1) Particulars and Details

The Shelburne Museum is a delightful place to visit. It is an outdoor museum in a shallow bowl of meadowland with the Green Mountains rising in the distance. The entrance to the Museum is a covered bridge across a little brook and through a thicket of vines and bushes to a parking lot, discreetly hidden by a grove of trees. It is a museum in the fields broken by little dips and rises and by groves of trees with picnic tables and fireplaces for the visitors. A narrow road runs around the field like a belt, and on it runs an open truck with a low platform and a row of benches on either side, proceeding so slowly that passengers can hop off and on with ease, or they can wait for it to stop at one of the designated stations. Scattered in the fields, none very far from the road and the little truck, are the exhibits: an inn, several houses with their original furnishings, and a prison with stocks—all from the Colonial period; a general store, of course; a one-room schoolhouse from grandfather's day; another store crowded with antique clocks and music boxes and mechanical toys; a nineteenth-century steam locomotive, and best of all, perhaps, the last ferryboat to ply Lake Champlain. It is a strange sensation to see the old side-wheeler landlocked on the side of a small hill, and stranger still to stand on its deck and look out over acres of greenery. One feels, perhaps, a little like Noah when the ark came to rest, at last, on Mount Ararat.

[In this paragraph, details about the appearance of the Museum and its exhibits are presented to develop the initial statement that the Shelburne Museum is a delightful place to visit.]

(2)   Instances and Examples

His life has been a series of brilliant ideas, early successes, and ultimate failures. His experience with diaper service is typical. He was the first to think of a laundry that would supply mothers with diapers and wash them for a reasonable fee. He worked out all of the details, including the container to hold the soiled diapers. He secured financial backing, organized a company, and directed its initial operations. But as the service took hold and the company began to make larger profits, he lost interest. The activity was no longer novel; the necessary supervision, the close attention to detail, became onerous. His mind was already occupied with another idea and another promotional campaign. Inevitably the customers dwindled, and so did the profits before the onslaught of other companies offering better service. His backers warned and complained and finally removed him from control. He left without regret and with only a little money that he was ready to invest in another idea, more brilliant than the last, that would make him a millionaire.

[Here the initial statement about the pattern of his life is illustrated by the example of the diaper service.]

(3)   Logical Divisions—Reasons, Classes, Steps in a Process

It [*The Impressions and Reflections of a Superannuated Man* by Sir Francis Denby-Johns] is, rather, three books in one. The first is a romantic and fascinating account of the young explorer (fresh impressions and impromptu judgments from the entries in his diary during the early years). The next presents the reminiscent Denby-Johns (reflective commentaries, "fillers," explanations and revisions of the original entries.) The third book may be said to consist of Langsam's narrative and interpretive connectives. *The Impressions and Reflections of a Superannuated Man* contains fewer entries from the diaries than did *Fair Horizons* and is consequently less interesting than that volume to the general reader and more interesting to students of archeology and ethnology.

[In this paragraph the book being reviewed is shown to consist of three parts or kinds of material.]

(4) Comparison and Contrast

The harpsichord is the most important forerunner of the piano. The harpsichord is somewhat smaller and more delicate than a grand piano, but looks like a grand piano except that it is tail-shaped rather than rounded or curved. Whereas the piano has only one keyboard, the harpsichord has two. Like the piano, the harpsichord has several strings to a key, but the strings of the harpsichord are vibrated by the plucking action of jacks rather than by the striking of hammers, as in the piano. The strings of the piano are controlled by dampers and pedals, but in a harpsichord the strings are controlled by stops, similar to those of an organ. Compared to the piano, the harpsichord is rather weak in tone and tinny; it cannot jump abruptly around the keyboard, and it is not capable of strong accents. On the other hand, the harpsichord can make more sounds to a key and is capable of such a variety of sounds that it frequently seems to be two different instruments. The harpsichord is different from a piano, but not inferior to it. For the music of its day, the music composed for it, the harpsichord is unequalled.

[In this paragraph the harpsichord is explained by means of comparison with the more familiar piano. The explanation proceeds by showing how the harpsichord is similar to the piano and different from it.]

(5) Analogy

Jane Eyre, who had been an ardent, expectant woman—almost a bride—was a cold, solitary girl again:

her life was pale; her prospects were desolate. A Christmas frost had come at midsummer; a white December storm had whirled over June; ice glazed the ripe apples, drifts crushed the blowing roses; on hay-field and corn-field lay a frozen shroud: lanes which last night blushed full of flowers, to-day were pathless with untrodden snow; and the woods, which twelve hours since waved leafy and fragrant as groves between the tropics, now spread, waste, wild, and white as pine-forests in wintry Norway.

[Here Charlotte Brontë uses the analogy of the effects of unexpected, unseasonable winter weather to describe the effect of unexpected emotional shock.]

(6) Definition

In the following paragraph, written by Lord Chesterfield to his son, the term *orator* is defined by both what the term means and what it does not mean.

Cicero, conscious that he was at the top of his profession (for in his time Eloquence was a profession), in order to set himself off, defines, in his Treatise *de Oratore*, an orator to be such a man as never was, or never will be; and by this fallacious argument, says, that he must know every art and science whatsoever, or how shall he speak upon them? But with submission to so great an authority, my definition of an orator is extremely different from, and, I believe, much truer than his. I call that man an orator, who reasons justly, and expresses himself elegantly upon whatever subject he treats. Problems in geometry, equations in algebra, processes in chemistry, and experiments in anatomy, are never, that I have heard of, the objects of eloquence; and therefore I humbly conceive, that a man may be a very fine speaker, and yet know nothing of geometry, algebra, chemistry, or anatomy. The subjects of all Parliamentary debates, are subjects of common sense singly.

(7) Cause and Effect

In *The Life of Addison* Thomas Babington Macaulay ascribes certain faults in Addison's character to the adulation of a coterie of inferiors with whom he surrounded himself.

> To the excessive modesty of Addison's nature, we must ascribe another fault which generally arises from a very different cause. He became a little too fond of seeing himself surrounded by a small circle of admirers, to whom he was as a King or rather as a God. All of these men were inferior to him in ability, and some of them had very serious faults. Nor did these faults escape his observation, for, if there was an eye which saw through and through men, it was the eye of Addison. But, with the keenest observation, and the finest sense of the ridiculous, he had large charity. The feeling with which he looked on most of his humble companions was one of benevolence, slightly tinctured with contempt. He was at perfect ease in their company; he was grateful for their devoted attachment; and he loaded them with benefits. Their veneration for him appears to have exceeded that with which Johnson was regarded by Boswell, or Warburton by Hurd. It was not in the power of adulation to turn such a head, or deprave such a heart, as Addison's. But it must in candour be admitted that he contracted some of the faults which can scarcely be avoided by any person who is so unfortunate as to be the oracle of a small literary coterie.

(8) Narration

The following excerpt from William Hazlitt's *The Fight* is an excellent example of a swift, vivid narrative paragraph.

> When the Gas-man came to himself, the first words he uttered were, "Where am I? What is the matter?" "Nothing is the matter, Tom—you have lost the battle,

but you are the bravest man alive." And Jackson whispered to him, "I am collecting a purse for you, Tom." Vain sounds, and unheard at that moment. Neate instantly went up and shook him cordially by the hand, and seeing some old acquaintances, began to flourish with his fists, calling out, "Ah, you always said I couldn't fight—what do you think now?" But all in good humor, and without any appearance of arrogance; only it was evident Bill Neate was pleased that he had won the fight. When it was over, I asked Cribb if he did not think it was a good one. He said, "Pretty well." The carrier-pigeons now mounted into the air, and one of them flew with the news of her husband's victory to the bosom of Mrs. Neate. Alas for Mrs. Hickman!

(9) Description

In the following paragraph from Thomas Hardy's *Far From the Madding Crowd*, Gabriel Oak's appearance is described in terms of the clothes he wore.

Since he lived six times as many working days as Sundays, Oak's appearance in his old clothes was peculiarly his own—the mental picture formed by his neighbour in imagining him being always dressed in that way. He wore a low-crowned felt hat, spread out at the base by tight jamming upon the head for security in high winds, and a coat like Dr. Johnson's; his lower extremities being encased in ordinary leather leggings and boots emphatically large, affording to each foot a roomy apartment so constructed that any wearer might stand in a river all day long and know nothing damp—their maker being a conscientious man who endeavoured to compensate for any weakness in his cut by unstinted dimension and solidity.

36C Suit the Length of the Paragraph to Its Purpose

The length of a paragraph should be determined by (1) the subject, (2) the fullness and completeness of development, and (3) the educational level of the readers. Modern paragraphs are between 100 and 300 words long, but there is no standard length for a paragraph.

Short, scrappy paragraphs should never be written. Paragraphs of one or two sentences should be used only as already explained. Comparatively short paragraphs are used for slight, simple topics and for larger topics if they are expressed in outline or only in essentials. Short paragraphs are also used in exploratory essays, in essays for the immature, and in swift, terse narration.

Longer paragraphs are used for larger topics and for smaller ones that are specifically and completely developed. Moderately long paragraphs are normally used in formal essays and in expository and narrative prose of leisurely pace. Excessively long paragraphs may be overloaded with details, or they may include more than one topic. The remedy for the first fault is to remove the unessential details. The remedy for the second fault is to revise the paragraph and limit it to one topic. If the paragraph is excessively long because it includes several aspects of one topic, the paragraph should be logically subdivided.

The beginnner can judge the length of paragraphs by the following rough tests:

(1) A paragraph of three or four sentences is probably too short. The thought may be incomplete; details may be omitted; necessary proof or illustration may be lacking.

(2) If a page contains three or more paragraphs, the paragraphs are probably too short and scrappy. Two or more of the paragraphs may belong together. Or all of the paragraphs may require more substance.

(3) A paragraph of a page and a half or more is probably too long. If it is overloaded with details, it should be reduced. If it

expresses more than one topic, it should be revised. Otherwise it should be logically subdivided.

(1) Short, Scrappy Paragraphs

A paragraph is a group of related sentences that develop one thought. A paragraph presents details or illustrations that give substance and meaning to one topic.

[This paragraph omits far too much to be a satisfactory definition of the paragraph.]

> An increase in the wages of steelworkers will be inflationary. It will force the steel companies to raise the price of steel. As a result, the prices of many commodities will rise, and our dollar will purchase less than it purchases now.

[This paragraph consists of flat statements without any reasons or explanations. Hence it does not tell the reader why and how a wage rise will be inflationary, nor does it carry any conviction.]

> Everyone who has a child in school should join the Parent-Teachers Association. The P.T.A. strives to improve our schools. It helps the pupils, the teachers, and the community.

[Without details to show how the P.T.A. tries to improve the schools and how it is helpful to students, and teachers, and community, this paragraph is weak and ineffectual.]

(2) Excessively Long Paragraph

> The fishing in Lake Queequee is excellent. The lake abounds with rock bass, black bass, small-mouth bass, pike, pickerel, yellow perch, white perch, pumpkin seeds or sunfish, bullheads, and eels. The pike, pickerel, and even the yellow perch grow big and gamey. They strike

the lure hard and they put up a fight before they are pulled alongside the boat and netted. It is not unusual to land a pickerel measuring thirty inches and weighing four or more pounds. Even the sunfish are big. Some are almost twice the size of a large hand. When they strike the bait and run with the line, the fisherman has to brace and pull hard. The sunfish bite all the time, morning and night and in the blazing afternoon, and in any kind of weather. Anyone can have a thrilling time just catching them, even the children. No sooner does a child drop a line in the water with a worm, without a worm, than a sunfish is hooked. In an hour's time one can catch a dozen or more. And the other fish, the pickerel and bass, bite, too, sometimes even for the children. Eventually even a duffer can catch at least one big, gamey fish to display and then to pack in ice and ship home for the family to admire. Night is the time for eels and bullheads. The hardened fishermen, mindless of mosquitoes and other insects, can always take their outboard motors and go to one of the many coves and there in the shallow water, among the weeds and wild rice that grow in abundance, catch eels and bullheads until the break of dawn. Then if they wish, they can fish for bass and pickerel and will probably catch them, too.

[The point of this paragraph could be made in half the length. It is not necessary, for example, to list all of the kinds of fish in the lake or to give so many details about how the fish are caught and how the fisherman gets to the fishing ground.]

36D   Make Your Paragraphs Unified

Unity is as essential in a paragraph as it is in a sentence. Unity means that a paragraph develops only one topic or one aspect of a topic. A paragraph is unified when (1) every sentence contributes to the development of the topic, (2) no sentence fails to advance the topic or introduces another topic, and (3) no sentence necessary to the development of the topic is omitted.

In the following paragraph the remark about the quality of coffee in lunchrooms has nothing to do with the diner's inability to get coffee and a sandwich at the same time. Hence this remark destroys the unity of the paragraph.

In luncheonettes it is almost impossible to order a sandwich and a cup of coffee and to get them at the same time. Usually the sandwich comes first, and the diner waits and waits impatiently for the coffee. Finally, as the last bite of food is swallowed, the long-lost waitress appears with the coffee. *Coffee in lunchrooms is uniformly bad. Either the quality is poor, or the coffee is weak and stale.* Sometimes the coffee is brought first. The diner waits hopefully for the sandwich as the coffee grows cooler and cooler. When the sandwich finally comes, the coffee is cold. Diners have tried every possible means of getting their coffee and sandwich together, but nothing works except luck—once in a blue moon.

The following paragraph by Henry David Thoreau is unified because every sentence, every detail, tells how Thoreau surveyed the country and considered every spot as a possible site for a home.

At a certain season of our life we are accustomed to consider every spot as the possible site of a house. I have thus surveyed the country on every side within a dozen miles of where I live. In imagination I have bought all the farms in succession, for all were to be bought, and I knew their price. I walked over each farmer's premises, tasted his wild apples, discoursed on husbandry with him, took his farm at his price, at any price, mortgaging it to him in my mind; even put a higher price on it,—took everything but a deed of it,—took his word for his deed, for I dearly love to talk,—cultivated it, and him to some extent, I trust, and withdrew when I had enjoyed it long·enough, leaving him to carry it on. This experience entitled me to be regarded as a sort of real-estate broker by my friends. Wherever I sat, there I might live, and the landscape radiated from me accordingly. What is a house but a *sedes*, a seat?—better if a country seat. I discovered many a site for a house not likely to be soon improved, which some might have thought too far from the village, but to my eyes the village was too far from it. Well, there I might live, I said; and there I did live, for an hour, a summer, and a winter life; saw how I could let the years run off, buffet the winter through, and see the spring come in. The future inhabitants of this region, wherever they may place their houses, may be sure that they have been anticipated. An afternoon sufficed to lay out the land into orchard, wood-lot, and pasture, and to decide what fine oaks or pines should be left to stand before the door, and whence each blasted tree could be seen to the best advantage; and then I let it lie, fallow perchance, for a man is rich in proportion to the number of things which he can afford to let alone.

36E   Use a Topic Sentence to State the Unifying Thought of the Paragraph

The topic sentence states the thought that the rest of the paragraph develops. The topic sentence usually appears at the beginning of the paragraph, where it marks the shift from the preceding paragraph and immediately announces the thought now being developed. In some paragraphs the topic sentence appears in the middle, or at the end where it may also act as a summary sentence. Some paragraphs have no topic sentence because the central thought is so obvious that it does not have to be expressed.

The beginner should start each paragraph with a topic sentence. In formulating the topic sentence, clarify the thought and fix the object of the paragraph firmly in mind. The topic sentence can be used as a gauge of what should be included in the paragraph. Details that help to develop the topic sentence should be included; details that do not help should be excluded. The topic sentence is therefore a prop and control which is needed by the beginner and may sometimes be dispensed with only after the principles of paragraphing have been mastered.

Observe how the following topic sentences succinctly express what the paragraph is about:

> *The mass of men lead lives of quiet desperation.* What is called resignation is confirmed desperation. . . .[*Walden*, by Henry David Thoreau]

> *No young man thinks he will ever die.* He may believe that others will, or assent to the doctrine that "all men are mortal" as an abstract proposition, but he is far from bringing it home to himself individually. ["On the Fear of Death," by William Hazlitt]

> *It is important to remember that, in strictness, there is no such thing as an uneducated man.* Take an extreme case. . . . ["A Liberal Education," by Thomas Henry Huxley]

> *The notions of the beginning and the end of the world entertained by our forefathers are no longer credible.* It is very certain that the earth is not the chief body in the natural universe. . . . ["Science and Culture," by Thomas Henry Huxley]

36F   Make the Paragraph Coherent

Coherence means natural or logical connection. A paragraph is coherent when (1) its sentences are logically arranged and connected, (2) the logical connection is clear and apparent, (3) the transition from sentence to sentence is easy and natural, and (4) the reader can see through the interrelationship of details and sentences to the purpose of the paragraph.

Coherence in the paragraph can be achieved in the following ways: (1) by the logical, orderly arrangement of sentences, (2) by the repetition of key words and the use of pronouns to refer to the preceding sentence, (3) by the use of transitional expressions, and (4) by the use of parallel structure (see Section 22F).

(1) Coherence by Arrangement of Sentences

The common ways in which sentences may be logically arranged are illustrated in the following paragraphs. The writer should choose the arrangement or combination of arrangements that best suits the material and the purpose.

TIME ORDER

The sentences of a paragraph may be arranged in order of time. Chronological arrangement is used in narrating action and in explaining a process step by step. In the following paragraph the temporary checks to American vitality are traced chronologically from the depression through World War II and the Korean War to the present.

> The vigorous climate for our national vitality has continued until the present. We have had our wars and depressions, but individual enterprise was not seriously challenged until 1929. In the next ten years we learned that progress is a myth, that business does not necessarily grow bigger and better, and that hard work does not always mean success. Then the Second World War taught us some new lessons; so did the Korean War; and so did the Russian earth satellite and the Vietnam War. Despite these checks, however, our tradition of ambition and aggressiveness remains, and our optimism has been only slightly dimmed.

SPACE ORDER

A paragraph may move from one place to another or from one direction to another. The arrangement of material in space is most useful in descriptive paragraphs. In the next paragraph, the theater off Broadway is traced from Greenwich Village to the East Side and then to Yorkville in New York City and thence south to Washington, D.C. and west to Los Angeles and San Francisco.

For purpose of contract, Equity has ruled that Off-Broadway is any place outside the area bounded by Fifth and Ninth Avenues and 34th and 56th Streets. In New York, therefore, Off-Broadway is Greenwich Village where the Theatre de Lys, the Cherry Lane, the Provincetown, and other little theatres are located. Off-Broadway is also the Lower East Side where, among several makeshift theaters, the Phoenix is supreme. Yorktown and the Jan Hus House are also Off-Broadway, and so is any other little theater outside the area prescribed by Equity. But the spirit of Off-Broadway exists outside of New York. It exists in the theater in the round in Washington, D.C.; it exists in Dallas, in the smaller groups performing around Los Angeles, and in the Actor's Workshop in San Francisco. Wherever small groups of professional players present plays that for a variety of reasons could not be produced by the so-called commercial theater, or wherever plays are given experimental productions, there is Off-Broadway.

ORDER OF CLIMAX

The details of a paragraph may be arranged in order of increasing importance. This is an effective arrangement because it builds steadily to a climax. In the following paragraph from Macaulay's essay on Milton, passages of Milton's prose are praised in ascending order as expressing the full power of the English language, as surpassing the finest declamations of Burke, as equaling parts of *Paradise Lost*, and as being an angelic chorus.

It is to be regretted that the prose writings of Milton should, in our time, be so little read. As composition, they deserve the attention of every man who wishes to become acquainted with the full power of the English language. They abound with passages compared with which the finest declamations of Burke sing into insignificance. They are a perfect field of cloth-of-gold. The style is stiff with gorgeous embroidery. Not even in the earlier books of *Paradise Lost* has the great poet ever risen higher than in those parts of his controversial works in which his feelings, excited by conflict, find a vent in bursts of devotional and lyric rapture. It is, to borrow his own majestic language, "a sevenfold chorus of hallelujahs and harping symphonies."

FROM THE FAMILIAR TO THE UNFAMILIAR

The explanatory paragraph below approaches the dialectical law of transformation through familiar facts about water and ice.

Everyone knows that most liquids become solid through freezing. As the temperature of water, for example, is decreased, there is no change in its liquid state. That is, water does not become more gelatinous; it does not become partially solid. Instead, at a certain moment water leaps from the liquid state to the solid one in one bound. This transformation of water into ice is a simple illustration of how, according to dialectics, quantity is transformed into quality and quality into quantity.

FROM THE GENERAL TO THE PARTICULAR

A paragraph may present a general statement and develop it with a number of details. The body of the following paragraph consists of a number of details that support the general statement, expressed in the topic sentence, that Sarzanno held religion in deferential regard.

Sarzanno was not as openly pious as Daniel Drew, but he held religion in deferential regard. At crucial moments he sought its comfort, and in his affluent years he was a ready donor to any religious denomination seeking contributions. During his long and dramatic bout with death and federal agents, he courteously and gratefully accepted a cross from a lay preacher who wished him well and the Sicilian wish for good luck spoken by some of his employees. "I know I need every bit of good luck I can get," he told his biographer. "I'm grabbing everything that comes my way." At different times during his life he swore that he was a Roman Catholic, a Jew, and a Protestant. He was buried as a Jew, but his mother was a devout Catholic, and as she viewed his body for the last time she tried to snatch away the prayer shawl in which he was mantled.

FROM THE PARTICULAR TO THE GENERAL

A paragraph may proceed from a number of details to a general conclusion. In the following paragraph a number of details about the constantly changing nature of things leads to the general conclusion that we never see anything as it really is.

The universe is in an unceasing state of change. The stars move eternally, expanding, cooling, and exploding. The earth itself changes: rivers alter their course, mountains erode, valleys deepen. Life changes through birth, growth, decay, and death. Even desks and houses and boulders are not inert, for at the microscopic level they are whirls of electrons. A desk looks today very much as it did yesterday or a century ago only because the changes in it have been too minute for our coarse perceptions. Matter looks solid to us only because its motion is too rapid or too minute to be felt. Our senses are so extremely limited that we have to use instruments such as microscopes, telescopes, seismographs, etc., to detect occurrences which our unaided senses are powerless to detect. Today even children know that there are vibrations we cannot hear and configurations we cannot see. Therefore it is ludicrous to think that we ever perceive anything as it really is.

(2) Coherence by the Use of Key Words and the Repetition of Pronouns

The repetition of important words in a paragraph keeps the reader constantly aware of the subject and binds the sentences together in a tightly unified whole. The repetition of pronouns helps to achieve the same effect and to make the thought flow smoothly from sentence to sentence. Note how the following paragraph is bound together by the repetitions that are woven through it.

> The disparagers of *culture* make *its motive curiosity*; sometimes, indeed, they make *its motive* mere exclusiveness and *vanity*. The *culture* which is supposed to plume *itself* on a smattering of Greek and Latin is a *culture* which is begotten by nothing so intellectual as *curiosity*; it is valued out of sheer *vanity* and ignorance or else as an engine of social and class distinction; separating *its* holders, like a badge or title, from other people who have not got *it*. No *serious* man would call this *culture*, or attach any value to it, as *culture*, at all. To find the real ground for the very different estimate which *serious* people will set upon *culture*, we must find some *motive* for *culture* in the terms of which may lie a real ambiguity; and such a *motive* the word *curiosity* gives us. ["Sweetness and Light," by Matthew Arnold]

(3) Coherence by Transitional Expressions

By showing the relationship between thoughts, transitional expressions help the reader to move from detail to detail and from sentence to sentence with a sense of direction and continuity. In addition to the repetition of key words and pronouns, coherence can be achieved by the use of the following transitional expressions:

ADDITION	In addition, again, moreover, further, furthermore, finally, lastly, at last, in conclusion, first, second
CONTRAST	but, however, yet, still, nevertheless, on the other hand, after all, for all of that, on the contrary, notwithstanding, it is true
COMPARISON	similarly, likewise, in like manner
PURPOSE	to this end, with this object, for this purpose
RESULT	accordingly, thus, consequently, hence, therefore, wherefore, thereupon
EMPHASIS	in fact, indeed, in any event, certainly
EXAMPLE	for example, for instance, thus, in this manner
SUMMARY	in brief, on the whole, in sum, to sum up, in fine
TIME	at once, immediately, while, meanwhile, at length, in the meantime, at the same time, in the end, in the interim, when, as, while
PLACE	near, beyond, opposite to, adjacent to, at the same place, here, there

In the following paragraph from "On the Physical Basis of Life," by Thomas Henry Huxley, the transitional expressions are italicized.

And what is this dire necessity and "iron" law under which men groan? *Truly*, most gratuitously invented bugbears. I suppose if there be an "iron" law, it is that of gravitation; *and* if there be a physical necessity, it is that a stone, unsupported, must fall to the ground. *But* what is all we really know, and can know, about the latter phenomenon? *Simply*, that in all human experience stones have fallen to the ground under these conditions; that we have not the smallest reason for believing that any stone so circumstanced will not fall to the ground; *and* that we have, *on the contrary*, every reason to believe that it will so fall. It is very convenient to indicate that all the conditions of a belief have been fulfilled in this case, by calling the statement that unsupported stones will fall to the ground, "a law of nature." *But when, as commonly happens,* we change *will* [sic] into *must* [sic] we introduce an idea of necessity which *most assuredly* does not lie in the observed facts, *and* has no warranty that I can discover anywhere. *For my part*, I utterly repudiate and anathematize the intruder. Fact I know, *and* law I know; *but* what is this Necessity, save an empty shadow of my mind's throwing?

36G Provide Transition Between Paragraphs

In addition to providing transition from sentence to sentence within a paragraph, the writer must also provide transition from paragraph to paragraph. Transition between paragraphs can be achieved by the use of a transitional expression or sentence. Transition from one major division of a composition to another may be achieved by the use of a transitional paragraph. A summarizing paragraph may also be used to show the relationship between the preceding and following parts of an essay.

(1) Transition Between Paragraphs

As a matter of fact, although few things are spoken of with more fearful whisperings than this prospect of death, few have less influence on conduct under healthy circumstances. . . .

On the other hand, religion has its own enlargement, and an enlargement, not of tumult, but of peace. . . .

You will see what I mean by the parallel of bodily health. . . .

Let us then put aside the scientific use of words, when we are to speak of language and literature. . . .

We now come to the Royalists. . . .

(2) Transitional Paragraphs

And now, what is the ultimate fate, and what the origin, of the matter of life? ["On the Physical Basis of Life," by Thomas Henry Huxley]

The foregoing remarks are intended merely as a prelude to a narrative I am about to lay before the public, of one of the most memorable instances of this infatuation of gain to be found in the whole history of commerce. I allude to the famous Mississippi bubble. It is a matter that has passed into proverb, and become a phrase in every one's mouth, yet of which not one merchant in ten has probably a distinct idea. I have therefore thought that an authentic account of it would be interesting and salutary, at the present moment, when we are suffering under the effects of a severe access of the credit system, and just recovering from one of its ruinous delusions. [From *Wolfert's Roost and Other Papers*, by Washington Irving]

The Writer's Approach to the Subject

From the novice with something to write comes the anguished cry: "How do I go about it?" Unfortunately for the novice there is no universal formula for writing. How a writer should go about a task depends on the subject, the purpose, and the readers. Every projected piece of writing is a new problem that requires its own solution. Nevertheless, there are general procedures and rules that apply to almost any kind of prose. The beginner guided by them should be able to produce an acceptable piece of writing.

The prerequisites for good writing are time and effort. The beginner should therefore be prepared to work hard but should not attempt to complete a paper in one sitting. Instead the task should be divided into logical steps which should be taken a few at a time until the work is done. With a simple, familiar subject the writer might, for example, determine the purpose and gather the material in one session, plan the paper in the second, and write and rewrite it in the third. More difficult subjects obviously require more time and effort and therefore more periods of work. The number of periods the writer devotes to the paper should, of course, be determined by the topic and by the writer's ability and temperament.

The advantages of writing a paper in easy, logical steps are obvious. Being spread over a number of periods, the task becomes less burdensome and painful. The writer brings a fresh, clear mind to each session. Each stage of the preparation leads to the next and makes it easier. In the intervals the writer gains perspective on the work already done and is therefore able to judge and improve it. The improvement is cumulative, and the result is a better paper.

37 Select and Adapt a Subject with Care

All writing begins with a subject. You may be required to write about a specific subject or one of several subjects, or you may, of course, be free to choose any subject you like. If you are fortunate enough to have free choice, you should be able to make the most of the opportunity, for success in writing depends, to a considerable extent, on an appropriate subject. But even if you must write on an assigned subject, you can lighten the task and increase the chances of success by adapting the subject to your own interests and sphere of knowledge. The first step to the successful completion of an assignment in writing, therefore, is to choose or adapt the subject wisely.

37A Choose a Subject That Interests You

The advantages of an interesting subject should be obvious. It makes the task of writing easier and pleasanter than it would otherwise be. An interesting subject induces an enthusiasm that the writer will in all likelihood communicate to the reader. The reverse is, of course, true. If the writer is bored, the writing will be leaden, and the reader will, in turn, be bored. Only a skillful writer can fake an interest and enthusiasm.

The subject should interest the writer. Generally speaking, you should not worry about the subject being of interest to others. Chances are that any subject of interest to one individual is also of interest to many others. And even a reader who finds the subject itself dull may yet enjoy the work because of the writer's enthusiasm. We have all had the experience of being fascinated by someone else's enjoyment of something that we do not like. "I wouldn't care for that," we say to ourselves, "but I can understand why she does."

There are, of course, numerous occasions when the writer must be careful to select a subject that will interest the readers. Whoever writes for a specific group or a specific occasion must select the subject accordingly. Of course, the ideal subject is one that suits both the occasion and the writer.

37B Choose a Subject That You Know About or Are Willing to Learn About

To write about a subject one must, of course, know about it. Knowledge is the substance of which writing is made. You can no more write an article without knowledge than you can knit a sock without yarn. In order to give the writing substance and conviction, the writer must have facts and opinions based upon facts. Knowledge of a subject gives a writer confidence and direction, whereas ignorance causes fumbling and groping. If the writer is ignorant, the writing will be worthless. If the writer is uninformed and vague, the writing will be uninformed and vague. Even minor omissions and mistakes are likely to invalidate the entire paper. Knowledge of the subject does not guarantee successful writing, but it is a necessary ingredient. Without it, failure is certain.

The student of writing should, therefore, select a subject that is familiar or one that is compellingly interesting. Knowledge can be supplemented in the usual ways: by examining the subject or reading about it, or by questioning others, or by a combination of these methods. The writer can also limit the discussion of a subject to a logical part that is already familiar. The matter of limiting and adapting a subject is discussed in Sections 37D and 37E.

In deciding what to write, the beginner should not reject familiar subjects because they are considered commonplace and dull. Usually it is not the subject but the treatment that is dull. Familiar subjects, those chosen from school, family, work, and social life, are the ones that everyone can write about most intimately. And they are subjects that everyone likes to read about, for the recognition of the familiar is one of the greatest pleasures in reading.

On the other hand, the beginner should not write about the bizarre and the adventurous unless he has experienced them. Otherwise, the writing will lack detail and verisimilitude. At best it will be vague, generalized, and totally unconvincing and uninteresting.

37C   Choose a Subject That You Can Write About with Honesty of Purpose

A writer should always express honest convictions and judgments and should not pretend to like things or to believe in causes merely because of an impression that the reader expects this. If you cannot write honestly about a subject, you should not write about it at all.

Moral reasons aside, writing dishonestly is writing against the grain. An experienced writer can make a case for something not believed in because of a mastery of the tools of expression and the ability to manipulate words and ideas with dexterity. It is difficult for any student of writing to determine opinions and express them clearly. You must first be able to express your own side of a question before attempting to write on other sides of it.

37D   Limit the Subject in Scope

The writer should select a subject that can be adequately developed in the number of words called for. If the subject is so slight that it must be padded, it should be rejected. If a broad subject cannot be logically reduced to the required limits, it, too, should be rejected.

Most subjects can be limited in scope. Some of the more usual ways of limiting a subject are listed below and are, for the sake of concreteness, illustrated with the subject of trade unionism.

TIME

The Origin of Trade Unionism
Trade Unionism in the Depression

PLACE

Trade Unionism in Salt Lake City
Trade Unionism in My Shop

COMPONENT PARTS

Trade Unionism in the Automotive Industry
My Union Local

ORGANIZATION

The Union Local
The Shop Steward

MODES OF OPERATION

The Strike as a Union Weapon
The Union Welfare Fund

DEFINITION

What Is Trade Unionism?
The AFL–CIO

CAUSE AND EFFECT

Why Labor Organized
Unions and Higher Wages

"The Origin of Trade Unionism" would require a monograph or a long essay, depending on the fullness of treatment. At the other end of the scale, "Why My Shop Should Organize" might be developed in a thousand words or less.

The writer may, of course, apply several limitations to the subject. A factual account of the Boston police strike, for example, limits the subject of trade unionism to an impartial narration of a particular strike action at a definite time in a specific place. "Why My Shop Should Organize" is limited to a definite time and place and, perhaps, to a few salient reasons why, under the circumstances, a specific group of workers should join a union.

It is not even necessary to cover a limited subject completely. The writer may, for example, further limit it by dealing with only the most important points and omitting the others. In George Bernard Shaw's *St. Joan*, for example, the Bishop of Beauvais reduces the indictment of Joan from sixty-four counts to twelve, saying that if she were tried on a great many issues she might escape on the great main issue of heresy. The great main issues are frequently enough to establish a case or make a point; the minor issues are often superfluous and are, sometimes, injurious because they seem to dilute the argument.

37E Adapt the Subject to Your Own Sphere of Interest and Knowledge

The subject should be adapted to the writer's own sphere of interest and knowledge. If, for example, the general subject is civil defense, you can write about the provisions for civil defense in your community or in your shop. With a broader knowledge of the subject, you might write about the inadequacies of the program and suggest improvements, or you might, from your investigations, oppose the program in whole or in part.

Many subjects can be adapted in this manner. They can be

discussed on the immediate and even personal level of home, school, or shop, or they can be discussed on a higher and more general level. No matter what the subject, you should discuss it concretely in an area with which you are familiar. You should, in a manner of speaking, cut the subject to your own size and tackle it on your home ground.

38 Determine Your Fundamental Purpose in Writing

The first thing a writer should do after selecting and adapting the subject is to determine the fundamental purpose. Almost any subject can be developed in a number of different ways. How it is developed depends on the writer's purpose. Take, for example, "An Account of Judge Mission's Record in Office." The purpose of this account might be to persuade people to reelect the judge or to defeat her. Or the purpose might be to present an impartial statement of the judge's record so that the voter can decide. And there might be still other purposes such as to state why the President should appoint her to the Supreme Court, or why Harvard should give her an honorary degree, or why she should be impeached and disbarred.

Since most subjects can be treated in different ways, the writer must decide at the outset the goals to be accomplished. Otherwise there is likely to be vacillation between two or more goals and thus, through irresolution, the production of a confused and pointless piece of writing.

On the other hand, if the writer states the purpose clearly, this creates a lodestone to keep the writer on course. With the purpose as a guide, the writer can decide what material to include and what to exclude because it is irrelevant or contradictory. The writer can decide what tone and mood to adopt, in what order to arrange the material, and where to place the emphasis. The guiding purpose is, in fact, the device a writer uses to bring every aspect of the writing into focus.

It is therefore good practice for the beginner to state the purpose in the following manner:

> I am writing an account of Judge Eunice W. Mission's record in office to persuade the voters to reelect her.

> I am writing this letter to persuade Johnson and Duckwith to take back the Chinese rug I purchased and to refund my money.

> In order to make the reader's blood run cold, I am telling this story about my narrow escape from death in the crash landing of an airplane.

> I am explaining how to cure meat so that the reader can, by following my instructions, cure meat at home.

39 Gather and Record Your Material

Once you have determined your purpose, gather and record the substance necessary to express it in writing. Material may be obtained from the following sources:

(1) From the writer's own fund of knowledge

From your own mind, cull every bit of pertinent information and jot it down, point by point. If you are familiar with the subject, you may not have to go elsewhere for material. If your own knowledge is not sufficient, however, supplement it with information from other sources.

(2) From observation and interrogation

You can obviously increase your knowledge of a subject by observation and interrogation. If you are writing about the condition or operation of something, for example, you can watch and examine it for yourself. If you are writing about how people are affected by something or what they think about it, you can observe them and question a representative number about the matter.

(3) From the literature on the subject

The most obvious source of information about a subject is what others have written about it. Newspapers, magazines, house organs, technical journals, and books are unfailing sources of information. To find the available information the writer should use the following aids:

1. The articles and bibliographies in standard dictionaries, encyclopedias, and histories

2. *The Times Index*

3. *The Readers Guide to Periodical Literature*

4. Bibliographies of the various subjects

5. Subject entries in the card catalogue of the library

6. The librarian

40 Make a Plan of Your Writing

All writing should be planned in advance. Planning a subject is thinking about it systematically. The plan is the writer's diagram; it is as necessary to the writer as the blueprint to the machinist or the pattern to the shirtmaker. Most bad writing is planless writing, writing that is aimless, confused, and even self-contradictory. Without taking thought, the writer sits down and writes, or tries to. It never occurs to the writer to think before writing. Yet that same person might make elaborate plans to spend a day at the beach or construct a radiator cover. To most people, writing is a mystery. It requires divinely inspired talent; either one has it or not and there is nothing that can be done about it. This is a mistaken notion. The ability to write effectively is no more mysterious than any other skill. It can be acquired by thought and practice. An essay and a radiator cover are made in the same way: by taking thought, making a plan, gathering the material, and then executing the work. Neither the radiator cover nor the essay may be a work of art, but they will be serviceable. And, of course, one will do better with practice.

To you the writer, the plan has obvious advantages. It means that you have analyzed your subject completely, patterned your material, and determined the following things:

1. Your fundamental purpose in writing
2. The major parts of your subject
3. The order in which the major parts should be arranged
4. The substance to develop each of the major parts
5. The arrangement of the substance in each of the major parts
6. The subdivisions and the substance and arrangement of them

If you are an author with a plan, you have thought the subject through. You know exactly what you want to say and how to go about saying it. You know where to begin, how to proceed from point to point, and where to end. You have built a skeleton and now need only to cover it with a fabric of words.

The plan simplifies the actual process of writing. Having planned your work, you do not now have to think about what to say, how to say it, and what to say next. Unlike the juggler who has to keep several objects in the air at the same time, you are now free to concentrate on only one problem—how to express your thoughts in words. You will not make false starts and contradictory statements, wander up blind alleys, or go around in circles. You will be able to write more quickly and more correctly. Solecisms in writing—incomplete and fused sentences, mixed and illogical sentences, disagreements—frequently result from confusion rather than ignorance. By eliminating the confusion, the plan reduces the number of solecisms, for the writer who has planned the work properly is not trapped into error. Having completed the draft, you will have to revise it, but you will not have to reorganize and rewrite it because of illogical organization or vital omissions.

All writing therefore requires forethought, and all but the simplest writing requires a written plan. The scope of the plan will depend on the subject. It should be obvious that the larger and more complex the subject is, the more detailed the plan must be.

The process of planning and writing an essay can be illustrated with the subject of our water supply. Let us assume that the writer has decided upon the purpose and expressed it as follows: to give children an easy, general explanation of how we get our drinking water.

From personal knowledge of the subject and perhaps from further study of it, the writer jots down the following items:

1. The reservoirs and watersheds
2. The protection of the watersheds
3. The prohibition of bathing, boating, etc.
4. The screens to filter the water
5. The ways the dams are constructed
6. The water tower in the stream
7. The pumping of water to the purifying station
8. How these pumps are powered
9. The cost of operating the pumps
10. The need for more reservoirs as a protection against water shortage
11. The huge tanks in the purifying station
12. The use of chemicals to purify the water
13. The settling of the impurities
14. The condition of the water at the end of this purifying process
15. The pumping of the water to another purifying station
16. The appearance of the hall
17. The use of sand and gravel to purify the water here
18. The central passageway

19. The reservoirs on the sides
20. How these filters operate
21. The layers of sand and gravel
22. What happens in this filtering plant
23. The checking of the filtering operations here
24. The corrective measures taken in the purifying station
25. The laboratory analysis of the water
26. The training required of the chemists
27. The equipment of the laboratory
28. The addition of purifying chemicals—chlorine
29. The pumping station
30. The underground pipes
31. The leading of water to the pumping station
32. The branching of the large pipes into networks of smaller ones
33. The laying and maintenance of this network of pipes
34. The pumping of water into houses by huge pumps in the pumping stations
35. The emergency water tower
36. How the water tower operates
37. What the water towers look like

Scrutinizing these items, the writer notes that despite the controlling purpose, irrelevant material has been included. The following items are therefore eliminated because they are not central to the purpose or would make the explanation too detailed and technical.

5. The ways the dams are constructed
8. How these pumps are powered
9. The cost of operating the pumps

10. The need for more reservoirs as a protection against water shortage

26. The training required of the chemists

27. The equipment of the laboratory

33. The laying and maintenance of this network of pipes

The writer also eliminates the following items because they are repetitious:

3. The prohibition of bathing, boating, etc.—because it repeats item 2, the protection of the watersheds

21. The layers of sand and gravel—because it repeats item 17, the use of sand and gravel to purify the water

22. What happens in this filtering plant—because it repeats item 20, how the filters operate

29. The pumping station—because it is sufficiently covered by item 31

Next, the writer scrutinizes the remaining items to see that they are in the step-by-step sequence required by the general process being explained. Since some of the items are not in proper order, the list is rearranged and renumbered as follows:

1. The reservoirs

2. The protection of the reservoirs

3. The water tower in the reservoir

4. The screens to filter the water

5. The pumping of the water to the purifying station

6. The huge tanks in the purifying station

7. The settling of impurities in the tanks

8. The use of chemicals to aid the settling process

9. The condition of the water at the end of the purifying process

10. The appearance of the hall

11. The central passageway

12. The reservoirs on the sides

13. The layers of sand and gravel

14. How the water is filtered

15. The checking of these filtering operations

16. The corrective measures taken

17. The laboratory analysis of the water

18. The addition of purifying chemicals—chlorine

19. The leading of water to the pumping station

20. The huge underground pipes

21. The branching of the large pipes into a network of smaller ones

22. The pumping of the water into the smaller pipes and up into the houses

23. The emergency water towers

24. How these emergency towers work

Although the items are now arranged in proper sequence, they are not arranged logically. There is no distinction between major and minor items; the relationship between the whole and its parts is not indicated. Consequently the writer now organizes the items to indicate these divisions and relationships.

   I. The reservoir and its protection
     A. The prohibition of bathing, boating, fishing, etc.
     B. The patrols to prevent violations

  II. The water tower in the reservoir
     A. Its underwater windows
     B. The screens to filter the filth
     C. The pumping of the water to the purifying station

 III. The purifying station with its huge tanks
     A. The settling of impurities in the water
     B. The use of chemicals to aid the settling process
     C. The condition of the water at the end of this process

IV. The next purifying station
   A. The hall
      1. The central passageway with its tile floor
      2. The reservoirs on the sides
      3. The layers of sand and gravel
   B. How the water is filtered
   C. The checking of the filtering process and the corrective measures taken
   D. The laboratory analysis of the water and the addition of chlorine

V. The pumping station
   A. The leading of water to it
   B. The pumping of water into huge underground pipes

VI. The network of smaller pipes in the cities
   A. The conduction of the water into these smaller pipes
   B. The pumping of the water up into the houses

VII. The emergency water tower and how it works

This outline is a topic outline. The writer may write a sentence outline, that is, express the major and minor items in sentences rather than in phrases and clauses. Some writers use paragraph outlines which consist of the topic sentence of each paragraph in the essay. The kind of outline the writer makes is of little importance. The important thing is that the writer plan the essay before writing.

41 Write the Essay from the Plan

Once you have made a plan and checked it carefully, you should follow it in writing your essay. You should write a series of coherent paragraphs covering all of the items in the outline in the order of appearance. If you think of a better arrangement while you are writing, you should not hesitate to make the change, for an outline is intended as a guide and not as a straitjacket. After an introductory paragraph the following explanation of how we get our drinking water follows the plan item by item.

THE WATER IN OUR SINK

When we turn on the faucet, water gushes out. Have you ever wondered where the water comes from and how it gets to the tap? And have you ever wondered what makes it so clean and pure?

Our water comes from lakes and streams. Some of them are natural bodies of water, and some of them are made by dams which force the water to collect in large reservoirs. These reservoirs are very carefully protected in order to keep them clean. No one is allowed to fish or swim in them or even to boat on most of them. There are guards to enforce these prohibitions and to see that the water is not contaminated in any other way. The guards prevent anyone from washing clothes in the water and dumping refuse in it. If the guards discover any violation, they report it to the authorities and arrest the violators.

In the reservoirs there is a huge underwater tower two or more stories high with windows through which the water runs. On the outside of these windows are coarse screens and on the inside are finer ones. These screens filter out twigs, leaves, paper, and other coarse objects, including fish, both live and dead ones. The filtered water then runs into a pumping station and is pumped to a purifying station.

The purifying station contains huge tanks in which the water moves very slowly. When brooks and rivers run swiftly, their currents carry off twigs, leaves, silt and other heavy matter, but when water runs slowly, the impurities sink to the bottom. This settling process is aided by chemicals which form large, white flakes upon the surface of the water. As these flakes sink, they carry impurities to the bottom with them.

When the water runs out of these tanks, it is only a bit cloudy and even seems to be pure. But if you were to examine it under a microscope, you would see thousands of objects swarming in it. These objects are bacteria. Since some bacteria are harmful, they must be removed so that they cannot make people ill.

In order that these bacteria can be removed, the water is pumped into another purifying station. This place is a large, light hall with a floor of white tile. Down the center of the hall runs a passageway; on both sides of it are small, square pools. The bottom of these pools is covered with slits through which the water runs out. Over these slits is a layer of gravel and then a thick layer of sand. The water seeps through the sand and gravel, but the bacteria and other dirt remain.

Of course, the bacteria are much smaller than a grain of sand, and the spaces between two grains of sand might just as well be an open door as far as they are concerned. What, then, keeps them inside the door?

This is what happens. As the water seeps through, it covers each grain of sand with a film of tiny water plants and bacteria. Other bacteria stick to this film as they are about to pass between the grains of sand. Strange as it seems, the bacteria themselves help to clear the water of bacteria.

While the water is being filtered, a man keeps watch. Wearing clean overalls and felt slippers, he walks up and down the passageway. He sees to it that the water is seeping through the sand in the pools at the proper rate. If the water seeps too slowly, the sand is dirty. Then the man closes some pipes and opens others. As a result, the water no longer runs through the dirty pond, but is sent into a clean one.

The water that leaves the hall seems clean, but it still contains some bacteria. In the purifying station is a laboratory where technicians examine the water to make sure that it is free of harmful bacteria. If any are detected, the director of the purifying station is immediately informed. He directs the river guards to find out why the water is contaminated and where.

In order to kill any bacteria that remain in the water, a technician adds a yellow poison called chlorine. The amount added is so small that the people cannot smell or taste it when they drink the water. But even such a small amount is enough to kill the bacteria.

Now that the water is thoroughly pure, it goes to the next station, a pumping station. In this station huge pumps force the water through large underground pipes. These pipes stretch for many miles and carry the water into the city. In the city the big pipe branches into many smaller pipes. The large stream of water is thus broken into many smaller streams which flow in all directions. Imprisoned in the pipes, these little streams flow into the houses and up to the top floors.

If you open the tap, the water gushes out. It flows with such force because large pumps at the pumping stations are constantly exerting pressure on it and forcing it through the pipes. Sometimes these pumps break and must be repaired. But even then the houses are not left without water.

For emergencies like this, water is kept in water towers. They are very big with round houses on the top and a narrow stairway winding up them. Inside there is a huge tank filled with water. The water tank is like a pond suspended high above the houses and trees. The tower is built so high in order that the water can be forced down with pressure great enough to force it up to the top floors of buildings. And so there is always clean, pure water for cooking and drinking, and even for bathing.

41A   Check the First Draft of the Essay Carefully

After you have completed the first draft of your essay, you should read it critically and make all of the necessary revisions and corrections. A draft has been properly edited when it meets the following conditions:

1. It corresponds to the plan, except for improvements made in the course of composition.

2. It is free of errors in grammar and structure.

3. It is free from errors in spelling, punctuation, and mechanics.

4. It is clear and logical.

5. It flows smoothly from paragraph to paragraph.

While revising the draft, you should read it aloud or have it read to you, for the ear often detects errors which the eye has missed. If you are uncertain, you may also seek the advice of someone who is competent to judge your work as a whole and to call attention to weaknesses and errors in it. However, you should accept suggestions only if you are convinced of their validity, and you should make the suggested changes yourself.

Anyone who is learning to write can profit by intelligent criticism, but not by having the work done by someone else.

41B   Write the Final Version from the Revised Draft

After you have revised your draft to incorporate all of the necessary changes, you should write your final version. You should then compare it with the draft to make sure that you have copied correctly and incorporated every change. Once again you should read the final version to be sure that it is free of error.

To be acceptable a paper must be neat and legible, satisfy the established rules for the preparation of manuscripts (see Section 45), and contain no more than three corrections on a page. Corrections should be neat and unobtrusive because an attractive paper commends itself to the reader.

42   Begin and End the Paper Properly

A paper should have a beginning, a middle, and an end. It should begin where the subject opens and end where the subject closes. It should begin by commanding the reader's attention and end when the argument is complete and before it is nullified or the reader is bored.

42A   Write an Opening That Is Suitable to the Article and the Anticipated Audience

Although there is no standard way to begin an essay, the opening must at least introduce the topic. One must not be expected to infer the topic while reading or to learn of it from the title. It is a convention that all articles must begin as if the title did not exist. An essay should not begin as follows:

EARLY MARRIAGES

Mother was twenty-six when she married father, and grandmother was married at twenty-four. But my sister Beth now wants to get married, and she is seventeen.

Although the title of this essay announces the topic, the opening does not. From the first three sentences the reader can merely infer that the essay is about marriage in general. A better opening would be:

EARLY MARRIAGES

Today early marriages are in vogue. My sister Beth is seventeen, and she wants to get married. At seventeen and a half her friend Sally is already married and pregnant. But mother was twenty-six when she married father, and grandmother was married at twenty-four.

Short essays and essays of moderate length on subjects of general interest do not, as a rule, require a formal introduction. The opening should introduce the topic and arouse the reader's interest. The art of the brief, striking introduction is illustrated by Charles Lamb's "A Chapter on Ears." The opening paragraph is:

I have no ear.

Hazlitt opens his essay "On the Fear of Death" swiftly:

Perhaps the best cure for the fear of death is to reflect that life has a beginning as well as an end.

Hazlitt also employs a swift, striking introductory sentence in "Whether Genius Is Conscious of Its Powers?":

No really great man ever thought himself so.

An introductory device that is frequently used to pique the reader's curiosity is the question. The model essay "The Water in Our Sink" in this section begins:

When we turn on the faucet, water gushes out. Have you ever wondered where the water comes from and how it gets to the tap? And have you ever wondered what makes it so clean and pure?

An essay explaining the origin and nature of the wind might also begin with questions and interesting statements as follows:.

> Do you think that invisible creatures exist only in fairy tales? Then look up in the sky. See the white clouds floating way up there? What is pushing them? The Invisible One. When it crosses a field, the wheat bows low to it; when it passes through a forest, the trees bend down their heads. In autumn it whirls the dry leaves down the street; in summer it beats up the dust and tosses it into people's eyes.
>
> You've surely guessed what it is by now. It is the wind, the invisible current of air that moves over the earth.

Another effective introductory device is the anecdote. Wilhelm Friedrich van Anspach's essay "The Early Flowering of Mozart's Genius" begins as follows:

> One day in Mozart's fourth year, Andreas Schactner, court trumpeter at Salzburg, accompanied Leopold Mozart to his home. There in his father's study they found young Wolfgang writing with a pen. He was writing a concerto for the clavier. Looking at it Schactner saw a daub of notes over dried ink-blots. He and Leopold laughed at the apparent nonsense. But then Leopold began to note the theme and the composition. Tears of wonder and delight filled his eyes.
>
> "See, Herr Schactner," he said, "how proper and logical it is, but it's useless because it is too difficult for anyone to play."
>
> "That's why it's a concerto," Wolfgang insisted. "One must practice it until he can play it." Then he played it, but only enough to show what he intended. And this was, as I have already said, when he was only four years old.

Some articles require a formal introduction. A formal introduction does more than announce the topic; it explains the purpose, scope, and method of the article. Formal introductions are used for long and complex reports and for investigations in which the reader requires preparation and guidance. Formal introductions may also serve to explain the pertinence of a topic and to justify essays on subjects which a reader, for a variety of reasons, might think ought not be discussed.

In his essay on "The Physical Basis of Life," Thomas Henry Huxley begins with a formal introduction because the discussion is somewhat technical and because he believes his ideas to be novel and somewhat shocking:

> In order to make the title of this discourse generally intelligible, I have translated the term "Protoplasm," which is the scientific name of the substance of which I am about to speak, by the words "the physical basis of life." I suppose that, to many, the idea that there is such a thing as a physical basis, or matter, of life may be novel—so widely spread is the conception of life as a something which works through matter, but is independent of it; and even those who are aware that matter and life are inseparably connected, may not be prepared for the conclusion plainly suggested by the phrase, *the physical basis of life*," that there is some one kind of matter which is common to all living beings, and that their endless diversities are bound together by a physical, as well as an ideal, unity. In fact, when first apprehended, such a doctrine as this appears almost shocking to common sense.

To explain why and under what circumstances *Walden* was written, and also to anticipate the charge of immodesty, Henry David Thoreau wrote a long introduction to his work:

> When I wrote the following pages, or rather the bulk of them, I lived alone, in the woods, a mile from any neighbor, in a house which I had built myself, on the shore of Walden Pond, in Concord, Massachusetts, and earned my living by the labor of my hands only. I lived there two years and two months. At present I am a sojourner in civilized life again.
>
> I should not obtrude my affairs so much on the notice of my readers if very particular inquiries had not been made

by my townsmen concerning my mode of life, which some would call impertinent, though they do not appear to me at all impertinent, but, considering the circumstances, very natural and pertinent. Some have asked what I got to eat; if I did not feel lonesome; if I was not afraid; and the like. Others have been curious to learn what portion of my income I devoted to charitable purposes; and some, who have large families, how many poor children I maintained. I will therefore ask those of my readers who feel no particular interest in me to pardon me if I undertake to answer some of these questions in this book. In most books, the *I*, or first person, is omitted; in this it will be retained; that, in respect to egotism, is the main difference. We commonly do not remember that it is, after all, always the first person that is speaking. I should not talk so much about myself if there were anybody else whom I knew as well. Unfortunately, I am confined to this theme by the narrowness of my experience. Moreover, I, on my side, require of every writer, first or last, a simple and sincere account of his own life, and not merely what he has heard of other men's lives; some such account as he would send to his kindred from a distant land; for if he has lived sincerely it must have been in a distant land to me. Perhaps these pages are more particularly addressed to poor students. As for the rest of my readers, they will accept such portions as apply to them. I trust that none will stretch the seams in putting on the coat, for it may do good service to him whom it fits.

The first paragraph of Harold S. Friedburg's article "You Can Take Good Pictures" explains the purpose and the method:

Even you can take good pictures. You can take good pictures without an expensive camera and elaborate equipment. You can take good pictures without first taking a course in photography. Let me tell you how. First I will tell you what equipment to buy. Then I will explain what a good picture is, and finally I will tell you how to take one. At the end of this article I will give a succinct list of instructions. Keep it with you, follow it, and you can't go wrong.

42B As a Rule, Do Not End a Paper with a Formal Conclusion

For most essays a formal conclusion is unnecessary. When the argument has been completed, the paper should end on a tonic note of finality.

A formal conclusion is used in a lengthy, complex exposition to state conclusions and to summarize points which the reader may have forgotten. In shorter and less formal exposition, however, a summary is superfluous.

Here is the end of Hazlitt's essay "On the Fear of Death."

> If we merely wish to continue our headstrong humours and tormenting passions, we had better begone at once; and if we only cherish a fondness for existence according to the good we derive from it, the pang we feel at parting with it will not be very severe.

42C Do Not Begin a Narrative Long Before the Incident Being Narrated

In narrating an incident the writer should begin with the circumstances in which it occurred and the events immediately preceding it. Do not begin with unnecessary explanations or remote and inconsequential events. An indirect or long-winded approach bores the reader and destroys the impact of the story. Furthermore, you may get lost in a maze of inconsequential details or exhaust yourself before you have narrated the climax of your story.

Suppose that Susan is telling how she and Steve were nearly drowned when they rowed into the ship's channel at Gloucester, Massachusetts, and their boat was swamped by a passing freighter. This story should probably begin with their taking the boat out. The writer can then concentrate on how, unthinkingly, they rowed into the channel and on the ensuing events together with their emotional reactions to them. The story should not begin with an explanation of why the couple decided to vacation in Gloucester. Nor is it necessary to say that on the preceding evening a guest at their hotel suggested the excursion, or even that they were eager to get out on the water because they had been kept indoors for three days by a northeaster.

Some representative beginnings:

> (1) At four o' clock in the afternoon we drove up to the gate of the Rocky National Park. Since the hour was late, I asked the ranger if we had time to cross Big Ridge into Estes before dark. [For an account of a harrowing drive over Big Ridge in a blinding snowstorm.]

> (2) When I was ushered to my place at the table, my heart sank. The woman at my left was Miss Tompkins. Ironsides Tompkins, the scourge of the Personnel Department! [For an incident leading to the revelation that the reviled Miss Tompkins is a woman of intelligence and charm.]

> (3) "I just talked to Tom on the 'phone, Ma," Iris said. "He'll be over this evening."
>
> Mrs. Sears laid her newspaper aside. "Like last Thursday?" she asked.
>
> "Well, not exactly like last Thursday. He just needed some help with a calculus problem then. He has something important to talk to you about, or rather *we* have something important to tell you." [This opening creates suspense, which can be prolonged as much as you think the reader will bear. Use your imagination to complete this beginning with an incident that is suitable.]

43 Adopt an Appropriate Mood, Tone, and Manner

In writing, the manner may be as important as the matter. An appropriate manner recommends what the writer has to say; an inappropriate manner may nullify it. In any form of writing, the manner should be appropriate to the subject, to the occasion and the reader, and to the writer.

43A Be Simple and Direct

Express the thought in language as simple as possible. Do not use learned, multisyllabic words if short, common words are as accurate and expressive. On the other hand, do not use several little words in lieu of a more expressive "big" word, unless you are writing for children, the uneducated, or the immature.

As a rule, approach the subject head-on. Do not write around it or come at it obliquely. Do not be coy. In other words, do not beat around the bush; come out with it.

Do not philosophize or pontificate about trivial matter. Only a pompous person or a fool will enlarge the magnitude of a thing and make a mountain out of a molehill.

43B Strive to Be Accurate, Clear, and Emphatic

Always ask three questions about every statement: Is it accurate? Is it clear? Is it emphatic? Accuracy, clarity, and emphasis are the essentials of effective writing.

Do not strive to display erudition or a large vocabulary. Do not strive to be original or poetic. Do not strive for style. Do not, in short, strive for "literary effect." Style does not come from posturing; it is the product of accuracy, clarity, and emphasis.

43C Be Modest, Unassuming, and Temperate

Do not pretend to know everything about a subject, large or small. Do not generalize from a limited knowledge of a subject. Having read only Sandburg among Lincoln's biographers, for example, do not say that Sandburg is the most reliable biographer of Lincoln. Say that Sandburg seems reliable. Above all, do not pretend to large knowledge in a subject you are just beginning to explore.

In a paper based on limited knowledge of a subject, do not be sarcastic, ironic, or otherwise scornful. Do not make accusations or judgments except within the limited area being scrutinized and then only with the greatest caution. Such arrogance and presumption are likely to be a boomerang.

Qualify statements and judgments. Say that things seem to be, or from your limited acquaintance appear to be. Say that in your opinion something is excellent; say that something is one of the best, or among the better, or it is the best that you know. There are numerous ways of qualifying a remark and avoiding the fatuous and irritating superlative.

43D Do Not Strive to Be Funny

Many students of writing have the false notion that the reader always wants to be entertained and that comedy is the only form of entertainment. The writer who is always striving to be funny is as tiresome as the guest who is always striving to be the life of the party. In writing, as in life, humor is a spice, effective when used sparingly.

If it be true that everything has an element of comedy, the person who always finds it is a bore. Serious subjects should be treated seriously. In them an accompanying patter of jokes and humorous comments is disruptive and offensive. And furthermore, the humor is likely to be forced and foolish. The writer should let the purpose be the guide. If the purpose is to explain, to instruct, or to judge, humor is out of place. This is not to say that the treatment may not, at times, be light, but it does not have to be funny, and the writer should not strain to make it so.

If humorous touches are appropriate or if the purpose is to amuse, the paper may, of course, be funny. Beginners should take warning, however; humor is one of the hardest kinds of writing. It requires a special gift and consummate skill.

44 In Descriptive Writing Use a Principle of Organization

Description is more than a catalogue of physical details. To make a definite picture and a definite impression, the details must be selected and arranged meaningfully.

44A Use a Fundamental Image to Help Make Description Graphic

A fundamental image is the basic form or outline of an object. For example, the design of a building is an *"H"* or a *cross;* Italy is shaped like a *boot.* The fundamental image offers several advantages. For the writer it provides a design on which to establish the position of details and show how they are related to each other. For the reader, it compares the object to something familiar which can immediately be visualized and to which the descriptive details can be referred.

The use of the fundamental image is illustrated by the following passage in which a street is likened in outline to a bent fishhook:

> Ours is really a one-sided street that curves partly around the village green like a *bent fishhook.* On the *shank,* screened by a row of poplars, sits the Williams Manse, now abandoned and boarded up. At the middle of the *bend,* flanked by neat cottages, is the district school. Diagonally across the green, on the *barb of the hook* sits

our house with a view of the green from the front porch and of the state highway from the rear.

44B Use a Fundamental Impression to Help Make Description Unified and Coherent

The first impression of anything is usually a fundamental impression. The observer perceives the object as a whole and makes an immediate judgment. Later, the details that contribute to the total effect are noted.

A fundamental impression is the total effect of an object. A kitten is *soft and cuddly.* A town is *rambling and squalid.* A room is *warm and cozy.* A day is *dreary.* Once you have stated the fundamental impression that an object makes, you can complete your description of it by presenting the details which create the impression. Thus the fundamental impression simplifies and clarifies the task of description. It is a principle according to which you can select pertinent details and around which you can arrange them. The fundamental impression is the purpose for writing the description.

In Herman Melville's *Typee* the fundamental impression of Mehevi is that of a superb-looking, imposing warrior. Note how this impression is stated and begins to take shape in the first paragraph of the description.

> At last . . . a superb-looking warrior stooped the towering plumes of his head dress beneath the low portal and entered the house. I saw at once that he was some distinguished personage, the natives regarding him with the utmost deference, and making room for him as he approached. His aspect was imposing. The splendid long-drooping tail feathers of the tropical bird, thickly interspersed with the gaudy plumage of the cock, were disposed in an immense upright semi-circle upon his head, their lower extremities being fixed in a crescent of guinea beads which spanned the forehead. Around his neck were

several enormous necklaces of boars tusks, polished like ivory, and disposed in such a manner that the longest and largest were upon his capacious chest. Thrust forward through the large apertures in his ears were two small and finely shaped sperm-whale teeth presenting their cavities in front, stuffed with freshly plucked leaves and curiously wrought at the other end into strange little images and devices. These barbaric trinkets, garnished in this manner at their open extremities, and tapering and curving round to a point behind the ear, resembled not a little a pair of cornucopias.

44C Use a Focal Point as a Means of Organizing Descriptive Detail

In description a focal point often helps the writer to arrange the details in a visual pattern. The focal point is usually the dominant feature of what is being described. The advantage of the focal point is that it establishes a center of interest, a fixed point which the reader as well as the writer can keep in mind and to which all of the other details can be related. The focal point pulls the details together and arranges them in a design that is readily visualized.

The use of the focal point is illustrated in the following description of a summer camp. Here the focal point is the main house, and the rest of the camp is related to it.

When I was a child, we spent our vacations at a fishing camp on Lake Obiscopee. The camp was situated on ten or twelve acres of pine land that curved like a broad ribbon around the lakefront. Above the lake in the center of the strip sat the main house. It was the dining room, the recreation room, and the office all in one, a haven where, on rainy days and cold nights, we played games in front of the large fireplace. From the porch overlooking the lake there was a piney view of the dock, the diving float, and the sandy beach where we children could swim unattended if there was a watcher above. Behind the main house stretched a large field, a good place to play ball or pick wild flowers and chase grasshoppers. The cabins were situated in the pines on either side of the main house, six on one side and five on the other, close to the lake and close to the dining room whither old Sam, the waiter, dishwasher, and general handyman, summoned us three times a day by rattling the cowbell on the porch.

45 Preparing the Manuscript

Neatness, legibility, and attractiveness of appearance should always be the writer's goals when preparing a paper to be submitted to an individual, a board or committee, a periodical, or a publisher. *Fair copy,* specified by most publishers, means a manuscript which is neat as well as correct. It is not required to be entirely free of erasures or corrections, but it is assumed that these will be held to a minimum and that there will be no difficulty in reading and no possibility of misreading.

Material of any sort submitted for publication should be accompanied by a letter. The letter need state only that you are submitting your work for consideration by the editor or publisher, or it may explain the nature of the work and point out any inducements for its publication, such as particular appeals for special groups of readers, the timeliness or importance of the topic, or any originality in your method of treatment.

45A Physical Appearance

The manuscript should be written or typed on paper approximately 8½ × 11 inches, the standard size of typewriter paper and commercial letterheads. It should be typed, if possible, and double-spaced throughout except for indented quotations, which may be single-spaced. (See 34B). If the manuscript is handwritten, lined paper should be used, the lines widely enough spaced to separate each line of writing clearly from the one above it and to avoid any suggestion of a cramped page. Whether the manuscript is typed or written, only one side of the paper should be used.

The first page should have the title at the top, followed by the author's name unless the manuscript is a report. Formal reports are concluded by the complimentary close *Respectfully submitted,* followed by the author's signature. Between the heading and the beginning of the text, extra space should be left, a line on ruled paper and at least a triple space on typewritten material.

THE CHANGING SEASONS
by
Arthur L. Kennedy

The advent of each new spring serves to remind us that Mother Nature has gone out of her way to see to it that we are not bored by any monotony caused by her. . . .

Indent the first and all succeeding paragraphs (five spaces is customary for typescript), but do not leave extra space between paragraphs. After the opening page, all pages should be numbered, preferably at the upper right-hand corner of each sheet. Page numbers may be placed at top center or bottom center of each page, but the upper right-hand corner position is preferable because it makes possible quick and easy reference to any desired page.

45B   Use and Position of Footnotes

Footnotes are a requirement for a research paper and are occasionally needed for other kinds of writing. They are used to acknowledge the borrowing of facts, statements, or quotations from specific sources. They may also be used for adding to the text explanations or supplementary material of any sort which is not sufficiently important to be included in the text or which would distract from the train of thought being developed in the text. If very few footnotes are used, they may be indicated by asterisks (*) or daggers (†), but it is usual and preferable simply

PREPARING THE MANUSCRIPT 195

to use Arabic numerals placed slightly above the line at the end of the quotations or statements for which references are given.[1] In a book of several chapters or other divisions, the footnotes may be numbered consecutively throughout the text, or a new numerical sequence may be introduced for each chapter or section after the first. If there are a great many footnotes, the latter method is preferable simply to keep the footnote numerals from reaching into the hundreds and consuming unnecessary space. As the name implies, the footnotes themselves are usually placed at the foot or the bottom of the page on which the indications are made. They should be clearly demarked from the text itself either by a solid line or by additional space separating them from the text. If the manuscript is to be submitted for publication, all of the footnotes should be placed together and appended to the text as a separate section. The printer will place them on the pages where they belong. (Footnotes are occasionally placed at the end of the article or book or at the end of each chapter or other division. This position makes the writing, typing, or printing easier, but it inconveniences the reader.)

45C Form of Footnotes—Primary Reference

When the first reference to a source is given, complete information about it should be included in the footnote (unless a bibliography is to be appended at the end of the work): the author, the title, the volume and edition (if there is more than one edition), and the page number. The place and date of publication and the name of the publisher should also be given.

> 1. John Macalister, *The Golden Gate,* 4th ed. (New York: John Horton & Co., 1914), III, 312.

This footnote indicates page 312 of Volume III of the fourth edition of a book entitled *The Golden Gate* written by John

---

[1]This is an example of an explanatory footnote. The footnote numeral always follows any punctuation occurring at the point of its insertion. The first word of any footnote is capitalized.

Macalister and published in New York by John Horton & Co. in 1914. If the volume does not contain a date of publication, the date of copyright is used. If no date at all can be found, the abbreviation *n.d.* (no date) is used. If no place of publication is given, the abbreviation *n.p.* means *no place.* Assuming these unusual circumstances for the above-mentioned work, the foot-note would read:

> 1. John Macalister, *The Golden Gate*, 4th ed. (n.p., n.d.), III, 312.

If a bibliography is to be added at the end of the work, only the minimum of information required to identify each reference need be given. The previous footnote would then read:

> 1. John Macalister, *The Golden Gate,* 4th ed., III, 312.

If the reference is not to a particular volume of a work, it is customary to insert the abbreviation *p.* for *page* or *pp.* for *pages.*

> 1. James Nelson, *Automation in the Textile Industry* (Chicago: Dunn & Co., 1959), p. 57. [or pp. 57-61.]

If there are two or more authors, their names should be listed as they occur on the title page of the book.

> 1. John French and Samuel D. Barton, *The New Dispensation* (Dublin: Standish & Sons, 1929), pp. 32–46.

If the source involves an editor or translator, this information should be given as follows:

> 1. William Shakespeare, *Hamlet,* ed. John Hurd (Boston: Alan Sims, 1870), p. 27.

> 2. Giovanni Boccaccio, *The Decameron,* trans. Ann Minter (New York: Dawson & Co., 1860), p. 47.

If the source is a collection of some sort which involves an editor only instead of an author, this information is conveyed as follows:

> 1. Thomas Diston (ed.), *Life Insurance Tables for Actuaries* (Cambridge, Mass.: The College Press, 1950), p. 68.

If the reference is to a source which occurs within a magazine, a newspaper, or as part of a larger work, the following usages are employed:

A signed newspaper article:

> 1. John Smart, "The Rising Tax Rate," *The New York Times* (February 8, 1912), p. 12.

An unsigned newspaper article (and indication of the section of the paper):

> 1. "The Rising Tax Rate," *The Memphis Star* (March 4, 1952), Sec. 2, p. 3.

A newspaper editorial:

> 1. "The Rising Tax Rate" (editorial), The London *Gazette* (April 7, 1936), p. 14.

A section of a book:

> 1. Jennifer West, "Search for a Father," *Thirty Famous Short Stories,* ed. Frederick Noble (New York: Eaton & Co., 1916), pp. 72-93.

An encyclopedia article:

> 1. "Textiles," *Encyclopedia Brittannica,* 9th ed., XXIII, 206–7.

[If the article is signed, the author's name should also be given.]

A story or an article in a magazine:

> 1. John Crow, "The Wayward Child," *The Atlantic Monthly* (June, 1944), pp. 8–11.

If the magazine has numbered issues, this information may be included, but the date should always be given if available:

> 1. Jennifer Finch, "The Golden Harvest," *The Farmer's Quarterly,* III, 3 (Autumn, 1940), pp. 36–48.

If the reference is to a speech or some kind of performance, all pertinent information should be given.

1. John Norton, "The Wavering Trust," sermon preached at the West End Tabernacle, Dayton, Ohio, Sept. 3, 1943.

45D Form of Footnotes—Secondary Reference

When exact reference has been made to a source, subsequent references (unless appearing after a considerable interval) may give the minimum of information required to identify the source. If a second reference is made to the same source and page immediately after the original citation, the abbreviation *ibid.* (*ibidem*—"in the same place") is all that is necessary. If the reference is to another part of the same work, the new page number, or the new page and volume number, should be added. Repetition of the identical reference:

1. Mary Watkins, *The Culture of the Aztecs* (Paris: The Little Press, 1914), IV, 27.

2. Ibid.

Reference to another part of the same work:

1. Mary Watkins, *The Culture of the Aztecs* (Paris: The Little Press, 1914), IV, 27.

2. Ibid., II, 423.

Ibid. refers always to the note *immediately above.* If the second reference to a source occurs after one or more intervening references to other sources have been made, the reference may be abbreviated to include only the author's surname and the page number.

1. Howard Lansing, *The Lost Cause* (New Orleans: James Sutton & Co., 1950), III, 27.

2. James Harlow, *The Opening Wedge* (Chicago: Little Books, 1912), p. 43.

3. Lansing, II, 134.

45E   Abbreviations

As a general rule, abbreviations of any kind should be avoided in the text of an article, but they are customary in footnotes and bibliographies. It was formerly standard procedure to put abbreviations of Latin or other foreign words in italics, but these abbreviations are so well-known that they may be said to have become completely anglicized. Consequently, the practice of placing them in italics has almost completely died out and will not be followed here.

The following are the most common abbreviations:

anon. "anonymous"—sometimes used in place of author of an anonymous work

art, arts. "article, articles"

b. "born"—used to indicate date of birth

bibliog. "bibliography"

biog. "biography"

bk., bks. "book, books"

ca. (or c.) *circa*—"about"—*c. 1909* means *about 1909*

cf. *confer*—meaning "compare"

ch., chs. "chapter, chapters"

col., cols. "column, columns"—for reference to the columns of print on a page

d. "died"

diss. "dissertation"

ed., eds. "editor, editors"—or "edition, editions"—or "edited by"

e.g. *exempli gratia*—"for example" (preceded and followed by commas)

esp. "especially"

et al. *et alii*—"and others"—as in a volume with many authors: *Smith, Houston, Jones, et al.*

et seq. *et sequens*—"and the following"

etc. *et cetera*—"and so forth"

f., ff. "and the following" line or page, lines or pages

fig., figs. "figure, figures"—usually referring to illustrations

fl. *floruit*—"flourished," followed by a date to denote the high point of an individual's achievement, principally used when dates of birth and death are uncertain

ibid., ib., *ibidem*—"in the same place"

id. *idem*—"the same"—used only in place of author's name

i.e. *id est*—"that is" (preceded and followed by commas)

infra "below"—used to refer to following material

introd. "introduction" or "introduction by"

l., ll. "line, lines"—used to refer to lines of poetry or similar text where exact reference is required

loc. cit. *loco citato*—"in the place cited"—in the place cited in a recent note

MS, MSS, MS., MSS., ms, mss, ms., mss. (capitalized or not, with or without period) "manuscript, manuscripts"

N.B. or n.b. *nota bene*—"note well"—to alert attention to what follows

n.d. "no date"—to explain failure to supply date of publication

no., nos. "number, numbers"

n.p. "no place" of publication given

op. cit. *opere citato*—"in the work cited"

p., pp. "page, pages"

par., pars. "paragraph, paragraphs"

passim "here and there"—used to indicate material that occurs here and there throughout a work

pseud. "pseudonym"

pub. "published" or "publication"

pubs. "publications"

sic "so"—usually placed in brackets to indicate that a seeming mistake is copied from the original work: *"It was thiers [sic]."*

trans. or tr. "translator" or "translation" or "translated by"

viz. *videlicet*—"it is permitted to see"—"namely" (preceded and followed by commas)

vol., vols. "volume, volumes"

vs. *versus*—"against"

45F Bibliography

Placed at the end of the work, the bibliography is usually the list of sources referred to in the body of the text or in the footnotes, or both. Sometimes, it may consist of works connected with the subject, whether referred to in the text or not. In either case, the listing is in alphabetical order and follows the plan for each entry of author, title, place of publication, name of publisher, and date of publication. If there is no author, the title of the piece is listed in its correct alphabetical position in the bibliography. If two or more works by the same author are listed, the author's name is not repeated, but succeeding titles by the same author are indented. For very well-known works like the *Encyclopedia Brittannica,* information about place and date of publication is usually omitted.

SAMPLE BIBLIOGRAPHY

Anderson, W. J. and Spiers, R. P. *The Architecture of Greece and Rome,* 2 vols. New York: Scribner, 1927.

Antcliffe, Herbert. "Music in the Life of the Ancient Greeks." *Musical Quarterly,* April, 1930, pp. 40-54.

Baker, Russell. "Kennedy Decries Big Soviet Gains." *The New York Times,* November 14, 1959, p. 10, col. 6.

Lee, Edwin A. "Vocational Education." *Encyclopedia Americana,* 1950, XXVIII, 160-161.

"Making Your Own Clothes." *The Young Lady's Magazine,* April, 1870, pp. 19-28.

Muir, Ramsey *The Expansion of Europe.* Boston: Houghton Mifflin, 1928.

—*Nationalism and Internationalism.* Boston: Houghton Mifflin, 1917.

Newton, A. P., ed. *Travel and Travellers in the Middle Ages.* New York: Knopf, 1926.

Rousseau, Jean Jacques. *The Social Contract* and *Discourses,* trans. G. D. H. Cole. London and New York: E. P. Dutton & Co., 1913.

45G   A Sample Research Paper

Although the material in this paper is drawn from an actual book, many of the references are deliberately artificial to illustrate different types of footnotes. The first two footnotes will assume that no bibliography follows the article. The remaining footnotes will give only the information required of footnotes when a bibliography is to be appended.

PRIMITIVE NUMBER SYMBOLISM
by
John L. Doe

Nothing in the history of number symbolism is so striking as the unanimity of all ages and climates in regard to the meanings of a certain few number symbols. Inasmuch as these same

number beliefs color the literature of the
ancient world and recur in the superstitions of
contemporary primitive peoples, we are justified
in classifying them as elementary or primitive
symbols.[1]

An examination of these earliest number symbols indicates that numbers originally carried
concrete associations, as a result of man's
early inability to comprehend abstractions.
Such a hypothesis is in keeping with the recognizable trend of language from the concrete to
the abstract,[2] and is demonstrable in the commonplace method of teaching addition and sub-
traction by the aid of concrete illustration.
These associations must originally have been
more real than the number itself, three trees
more real than the abstract number three, so
that particularly prominent and fixed numerical
groups might readily come to be thought of as
the attributes of the numbers themselves. In
ancient Babylon, as Cumont points out,

> a number was a very different thing from a
> figure. Just as in ancient times, and above
> all, in Egypt the name had a magic power,...
> so here the number possesses an active force,
> the number is a symbol, and its properties
> are sacred attributes.[3]

---

1. Cf. John D. Elder, Primitivism, Yesterday
and Today (New York: Hamlin & Co., 1943), passim.
2. Joyce Lermont, "Some Observations on Primitive Languages," The Linguistic Review (April,
1930), pp. 42-58.
3. Franz Cumont, Astrology and Religion among
the Greeks and Romans, pp. 29-30.

Presumably every early civilization once
passed through a stage today duplicated in certain Brazilian tribes whose languages are almost
completely barren of number words.[4] One tribe
uses only the word etama, alone, to indicate a
single object or one of a group. The first advance toward counting develops the use of words
for one and many, the differentiation of the
individual from the group.[5]

But man must soon have become conscious of the
duals of nature: male and female, day and night,
sun and moon. Doubtless Alcmaeon of Crotona was
repeating a very common observation when he re-
marked that "most human things go in pairs."[6]
It is probable, then, that the early mathemati-
cian chose some noteworthy duality of nature,
such as marriage, as his word for two. At any
rate, the number two appears always to have
carried with it the idea of mutual antithesis
found in the duals of nature, whether in the
great Manichean duad or in the double head of
the Egyptian Horus "whereof the one beareth
right and truth and the other wickedness."[7]

Having invented a term for "pair," man was in
possession of three numerical terms, one, two,
many, and there are tribes today who count in
just such a fashion.[8] Through some process not
clearly traceable, there came to be an identifi-

---

4. Levi Leonard Conant, The Number Concept,
p. 1.
5. Ibid., pp. 1, 22, 24, 28; Edward B. Tylor,
Primitive Culture, I, 243.
6. Aristotle, Metaphysics, I, 5.
7. Book of the Dead, XCII, 28.
8. Conant, p. 22; D. E. Smith, History of
Mathematics, I, 6, 9; Tylor, I, 243.

cation of the word for many with the concept of
three. This stage is reflected in the distinction between the dual and the plural in the
Egyptian, Arabian, Hebrew, Sanskrit, Greek, and
Gothic languages,[9] and in the common use of
positive, comparative, and superlative degrees.

The idea of three as implying the superlative,
or the all, was never lost. It appears in such
common phrases as ter felix ("thrice happy"), in
the use of the trident and triple thunderbolt as
symbols of greatness and power, in the Egyptian
hieroglyphs, where a single bar marking the picture of an object indicates but one, a double
bar two, but three lines indicate three or an
indefinite number of objects.[10]

The persistence of this half-instinctive mode
of reasoning is one of the curiosities of human
logic. Erastosthenes (c. 240 B.C.) observes
that "the gods vouchsafe moral improvement to
those who have thrice wiped themselves clean."[11]
Legends, myths, folk tales of all nations abound
in three wishes, three tries, three suitors--
there is no necessity for prolonging the story
when three is all. In the Old Testament we are
told that "a threefold cord is not quickly broken."[12] The medieval theologian makes a point
of the three days entombment of Christ, "for in
three days is proved all deed and fait verita-
ble."[13] Lewis Carroll was possibly hinting at

---

9. Tylor, I, 265.

10. Ibid.

11. Frederick Cornwallis Conybeare, Myth, Magic
and Morals, p. 318.

12. Ecclesiastes 4:12.

13. Legenda aurea, Resurrection (Temple
Classics), pp. 87-88.

the frailty of even modern scientific minds in accepting three examples as proof when he has the Bellman gravely announce, "What I tell you three times is true."

The triplicity of rising, midday, and setting sun provides another instance where three is all: beginning, middle, end. In the human cycle, to go no further in search of analogies, birth, life, and death represent the triple division which is common to all mundane affairs, recognized in the Greek Fates and the Scandinavian Norns. In Indian theology, Brahma, Vishnu, and Siva are similarly disposed. In a fragment of the Orphic theogony, Zeus is described as the beginning, middle, and end of all things.[14]

From early associations of this kind with specific numbers, there were gradually developed many different types of elaborate and complex number symbolisms, some of which died with medieval magic and various mystical cults but many of which survive to the present day.

---

14. Eduard Zeller, A History of Greek Philosophy, I, 64.

Glossary of Words and Phrases Frequently Misused

G1   a, an   Use *a* before words beginning with a consonant sound: *a book, a unique necklace.* Use *an* before words beginning with a vowel sound: *an apple, an urchin.* NOTE: It is the sound, not the actual letter which determines the form of the indefinite article: *a university, an R.C.A. television set, an 8-sided object.*

G2   accept, except   *Accept* means to receive: "Please *accept* my offer." The verb *except* means to leave out: "Will you *except* the last provision of the contract?"

G3   adapt, adopt   *Adapt* incorporates the word *apt,* which means *suited to the purpose;* therefore, *adapt* means *to make suitable. Adopt* means *to choose* or *to make one's own selection.* "We *adopted* the style of play which had been *adapted* from the style used by the Green Bay Packers."

G4   adverse, averse   *Adverse* means *opposing: adverse circumstances. Averse* means *disinclined:* "He was *averse* to my proposal." *Adverse* is usually related to actions or things, *averse* to people (who have an aversion).

207

G5   **advert, avert**   *Advert* means *refer:* "*The speaker adverted* to an earlier talk he had given." *Avert* means *ward off:* "He narrowly *averted* a bad fall."

G6   **affect, effect**   *Affect* means *to influence:* "His attitude in class *affected* his grade." *Affect* is never used as a noun except in psychological terminology. *Effect* as a noun means *result:* "The *effect* of the explosion was disastrous." *Effect* as a verb means *to accomplish:* "The new machinery *effected* a decided improvement in the product."

G7   **aggravate**   Do not use *aggravate* to mean *irritate. Aggravate* means to make a bad situation worse.

G8   **alright**   A bad spelling of *all right.* Do not confuse the spelling with words like *almost, already, altogether.*

G9   **alumnus, alumna, alumni, alumnae**   An *alumnus* is a male graduate. *Alumni* is the plural. An *alumna* is a female graduate. *Alumnae* is the plural. *Alumni* is used for male and female combined.

G10   **amend, emend**   *Amend* means to alter for the better, as in *amendments* to the Constitution. *Emend,* once an alternative spelling for *amend,* now is specialized in use to mean removing errors from a text.

G11   **amiable, amicable**   *Amiable* is used to describe persons who are kind, gentle, and friendly. *Amicable* is used to describe arrangements or settlements which are agreed to peacefully by both parties.

G12   **among, between**   *Between* is used in connection with two persons or things. "He divided the money *between* his two sons." *Among* is used for more than two: "He divided the money *among* his three sons." EXCEPTIONS: If more than two are involved in a united situation, *between* is used: "*Between* the four of us we raised a thousand dollars." If a comparison or an opposition is involved, *between* is used: "There was great rivalry *between* the three colleges. It was difficult to choose *between* them."

G13   **amount, number**   *Amount* refers to bulk or quantity: *amount* of sugar, grain, flour, money. *Number* refers to objects which are thought of as individual units; *number* of oranges, children, diamonds. Notice that most words following *amount* are singular (*coal, butter, water*) and that most words following *number* are plural (*apples, bottles, cups*).

G14 **and/or** Although the legalism *and/or* is becoming common in current English, it is to be avoided as faddish verbiage. The simple word *or* carries exactly the same meaning in most cases and does not call attention to itself.

G15 **ante-, anti-** These prefixes, though similar, are quite different in meaning. *Ante-* means *before,* as in *antechamber* (a small room that comes before a larger one) or *antebellum* (before the war). *Anti-* means opposed to, as in *anti-nuclear* or *antitoxin.*

G16 **apt, liable, likely** *Apt* refers to a habitual disposition: "Having a good brain, he is *apt* to get high grades." *Likely* merely expresses probability: "It is *likely* to rain." *Liable* implies the probability of something unfortunate: "The firm is *liable* to fail."

G17 **as, like** When used as a preposition, *like* should never introduce a clause (NOT *like I was saying*). When introducing a clause, *as* is used (*as I was saying*) even if some of the words of the clause are implied: "He did it as well *as* I [did]." (See 6A.)

G18 **beside, besides** *Beside* means *by the side of:* "Ask him to sit *beside* me." *Besides* means *in addition:* "She had an apartment in the city. *Besides,* she owned a home at the shore."

G19 **bring, take** *Bring* refers to action toward the writer or speaker: "*Bring* the book to me." *Take* refers to action away from the writer or speaker: "When you leave us, *take* your books with you."

G20 **burst, bust** *Burst,* meaning to explode or erupt from inward pressure, is sometimes written *bust,* but this is slang and is incorrect.

G21 **can, may** *Can* implies ability: "I *can* (I am able to) swim." *May* denotes permission: "*May* I (Have I permission to) swim in your pool?" In informal speech, when the context is clear, *can* and *may* are both used to express permission. (See 3G.)

G22 **claim, assert** *Claim* refers to a justified demand or legal right: "I *claim* this piece of property." "I *claim* the prize." It should not be used when only an assertion is involved; "He *asserted* (not *claimed*) that his demands were reasonable."

G23 compare to, compare with *Compare to* is used to indicate a definite resemblance: "He compared the railroad *to* a street." *Compare with* is used to indicate an examination of similarities and dissimilarities: "He compared the middle ages *with* modern times."

G24 complement, compliment A *complement* is something that fills up or completes, as in the sentence: "Foreign travel is a *complement* to the study of geography." A *compliment* is, of course, an expression of praise, as in "He paid her a high *compliment*." For some reason, compliments are "paid" and, in fact, should be properly earned or left unstated.

G25 consensus Even in respected newspapers, *consensus* is sometimes misspelled "concensus," perhaps in the mistaken idea that a "census" has been taken to determine agreement. The root word has to do with consent, hence *consensus*. Do not use the phrase *consensus of opinion,* which is redundant.

G26 counsel, council *Counsel* as a noun means *advice,* or, in legal parlance, a lawyer or lawyers: "He sought my *counsel*." "He retained *counsel* to represent him at the trial." As a verb *counsel* means to *advise:* "I would *counsel* you to accept the first good offer." *Council* is a *group* of individuals who act in advisory capacity or who meet for the purposes of discussion or decision-making: "The mayor met with the *council*." "They called a *council* to make plans for the future."

G27 detract, distract Although both of these words mean to draw away from, *detract* has come to mean taking away someone's good name, as in "His constant lying *detracts* from his good qualities." *Distract* means drawing the mind away from whatever it had been thinking, as in "The loud noise *distracted* her, making her lose concentration."

G28 different from *Different from* is the correct idiom, NOT *different than.*

G29 differ from, differ with *Differ from* applies to differences between one person or thing and others: "My car *differs from* his because it is a newer model." *Differ with* means to have a difference in opinion: "*I differ with* him in his views about government."

G30 discreet, discrete *Discreet* means careful in avoiding mistakes, as in "He was *discreet* in his habits." *Discrete* means separate, or detached, as in "Each grain of rice was *discrete,* not clinging to the rest in a glutinous mass."

G31 disinterested, uninterested *Disinterested* means impartial, showing no preference or prejudice. To be *uninterested* is to be bored, or simply lacking interest.

G32 don't *Don't* is the contraction of *do not: I don't, you don't, we don't, they don't.* Do not confuse it with *doesn't,* the contraction of *does not: He doesn't, she doesn't, it doesn't.*

G33 due to *Due to* functions like the adjective *attributable* plus the preposition *to.* "The *flood* was *attributable to* the rapid spring thaw." "The *flood* was *due to* the rapid spring thaw." If there is no noun like *flood* for the adjective *due to* to refer to, use the preposition *because of:* "He was late *because of* an accident." Or rephrase the sentence: "His *lateness* was *due to* an accident."

G34 fewer, less *Fewer* is used in connection with people or with objects which are thought of as individual units: *fewer oranges, fewer children, fewer books, fewer dollars. Less* is used in connection with the concept of bulk: *less money, less coal, less weight, less grain.* Notice that most words following *fewer* are plural (*oranges, books, dollars*); most words following *less* are singular (*money, coal, wheat*).

G35 forceful, forcible One can have a *forceful* personality, but to break down a door violently is to make a *forcible* entry.

G36 former, latter *Former* and *latter* are used to designate one of *two* persons or things: "Of the *two* possibilities, I prefer the *former* to the *latter.*" If more than two persons or things are involved, *first* or *first named* and *last* or *last named* are used: "He had a choice of yellow, rose, pink, and brown. He preferred the *first* and *last* to the others."

G37 fortuitous That which is *fortuitous* happens by accident and may or may not be a favorable event. The word is often misused as a synonym for *fortunate,* but it does not have this meaning.

G38 had ought *Ought* is known as a defective verb because it has only one form and cannot be used with an auxiliary: "They *ought* (NOT *had ought*) to have told her."

G39 hanged, hung *Hanged* is used in connection with executions: "He was condemned to be *hanged* by the neck until dead." *Hung* denotes any other kind of suspension: "The pictures were *hung* on the wall."

G40 **hardly** Like *barely* and *scarcely*, *hardly* should not be used with a negative. "He was *hardly* (*barely*, *scarcely*) able to do it." (NOT *not hardly, barely, scarcely*)

G41 **healthful, healthy** *Healthful* means *health-giving: a healthful climate. Healthy* means *in a state of health:* "He was a *healthy* young man."

G42 **imply, infer** *Imply* means to throw out a hint or suggestion: "She *implied* by her manner that she was unhappy." *Infer* means to take in a hint or suggestion: "I *inferred* from her manner that she was unhappy."

G43 **invaluable, priceless** Usually, the prefix *in-* indicates a negative, but *invaluable* does not mean "of no value." It means that the value of the object is so great that its worth cannot be evaluated. The word *priceless* has the same meaning: "so great a value that a price cannot be set for it."

G44 **its, it's** *Its* (no apostrophe) is the possessive case of *it:* "The pig nursed *its* young." *It's* is the contraction for *it is:* "*It's* too late to do anything about it."

G45 **kind, sort, type, variety** Since these words are singular in number, they should never be prefaced by plural demonstrative pronouns: *This kind of people* (NOT *these kind of people*).

G46 **kind of, sort of, type of, variety of** Never use *a* or *an* after these expressions. *Kind of a pistol* is confusing because *a* is used for one particular member of a class; whereas *kind of pistol* is preferable because *pistol* by itself correctly refers to the general idea of *pistol*.

G47 **lay, lie** *Lay, laid, laid* are the principal parts of the transitive verb which means *to put down:* "I shall *lay* the rug." I *laid* the rug." "I *have laid* the rug." *Lie, lay, lain* are the principal parts of the intransitive verb (it cannot take an object) which means *to recline* or *repose:* "She *will lie* in the hammock." She *is lying* in the hammock." She *lay* in the hammock yesterday." "She *has lain* there all afternoon."

G48 **lead, led** When pronounced alike, the noun *lead* is the metal, *led* is the past tense and past participle of the verb *to lead*.

G49   **learn, teach**   *Learn* means to acquire information or knowledge: "I *learned* my lesson." *Teach* means to impart information or knowledge: "I *taught* him to do it."

G50   **liable**   See *apt* (G16).

G51   **like**   See *as* (G17).

G52   **militate, mitigate**   *Militate* (connected with *military*) means to have strong influence for or against, usually against: "His grouchy manner *militated* against his success as a salesman." *Mitigate* means to *lessen:* "The cold compress on his leg *mitigated* his suffering."

G53   **myself**   *Myself* (like *yourself, himself, herself, itself, themselves*) is an intensive and reflexive pronoun. It should never be used in a sentence without its corresponding noun or pronoun: "I *myself* will do it." "*I hurt myself.*" "They sent for John and *me* (NOT *myself*)." (See 2F.)

G54   **principal, principle**   *Principal* is usually an adjective: *principal cities, principal people*. It has become a noun in a few usages where the noun it formerly modified has been dropped. "He was the *principal* (teacher) of the school." "I withdrew the *principal* (amount) and interest from my savings account." "He acted as the *principal* (person) rather than as an agent." In every other usage, the noun *principle* means a basic law or doctrine: "The country was founded on the *principle* that all men are created equal."

G55   **reason is because**   The words *reason is* (*was,* etc.) should be followed by a statement of the reason: "The reason for his failure was illness." "The reason for the strict rules is to enforce discipline." Similar statements can be made by using *because:* "He failed because of illness." "The rules are strict because it is necessary to enforce discipline." *Reason* and *because* convey the same sense. It is illogical to use both words to convey the same meaning.

G56   **respectable, respectful**   *Respectable* means "worthy of respect or esteem," as in "She had a *respectable* command of the German language." *Respectful* means "showing respect for something else," as in "The teacher received the *respectful* attention of the class." Many letters are closed with "*Respectfully* yours."

G57   **same**   Do not use *same* as a pronoun: "I have your order for the books and will send *them* (NOT will send *same*)."

G58   **their, there**   Be careful to distinguish the spelling of the possessive case of the pronoun *their (their books)* from the spelling of the adverb and the expletive *there.* "I got *there* before I knew it." "*There* are forty grapefruit in the crate."

G59   **therefor, therefore**   *Therefor* means *for that, for it, for them:* "I sent the manuscript by registered mail and have the receipt *therefor.*" *Therefore* means *for that reason:* "He was sick. *Therefore* he did not go to work."

G60   **unique**   *Unique* means the only one of its kind: "His was a *unique* personality." It cannot logically be used in a comparative or superlative form. Something may be more or most odd, rare, unusual, peculiar, remarkable, etc., but NOT more or most unique.

G61   **who's, whose**   *Who's* is the contraction for *who is* and *who has:* "I cannot imagine *who's* coming." *Whose* is the possessive form of *who:* "We knew the family *whose* house was robbed."

G62   **woman, women**   Just as the plural of *man* is *men,* so the plural of *woman* is *women.*

Which Prepositions Go with Which Verbs?

Prepositions are necessary words because they show the spatial or temporal relationships between physical things. But one problem in using prepositions is choosing the appropriate one to go with certain verbs. Most of the time there is no problem, and we know what is meant when someone says, "He was with the car" or "He was in the car" But it is more difficult when we consider the subtle choice between "He spoke with anger" or "He spoke in anger."

In many cases, however, certain idiomatic combinations of verbs and prepositions have been firmly established in the language, and these should be respected. For example, we can say *agree to,* but not *agree at,* and *decide on,* but not *decide in.* More than likely, when a certain preposition sounds more familiar in a given context than another preposition, the more familiar one is the better. The following discussion of various prepositions includes many of the troublesome idiomatic combinations.

Pl   about   The preposition *about* sometimes means *around* or *circling,* as in "He walked *about* the town." It also sometimes means *approximately,* as in "She came *about* six o'clock." With a compound verb, the use of *about* weakens the sentence and makes it less precise: "I had forgotten that" is stronger than "I had forgotten *about* that."

P2 **at, in** These prepositions can sometimes be used interchangeably, with resulting slight differences in meaning. "The meeting was held *at* the church" and "The meeting was held *in* the church" mean virtually the same thing. "She is *at* the theater" suggests that she is a spectator at a play, but "She is *in* the theater" could indicate that she is in the building or that she is an actress in the profession of acting. The word *in* is used in reference to cities; normally we say, "He is *in* Boston," not "He is *at* Boston."

P3 **by** The preposition *by* usually means *near,* as in "He was standing *by* the pond." When used with time, it means *not later than,* as in "I'll be home *by* midnight." With verbs of motion, *by* can suggest *to avoid* or *to ignore,* as in "He walked right *by* her," or "Death passed her *by.*"

P4 **for** There are many meanings of the preposition *for.* It can be used to show distance, as in "Walk *for* a mile" or time, as in "Wait *for* a year." It can also indicate destination, as in "We set out *for* Hartford." It can even mean that we favor something or someone, as in "We are *for* the mayor." Rarely does one have problems deciding which verbs to use with *for.*

P5 **in, into** Although *into* is sometimes used interchangeably with *in,* it can also be used to intensify a meaning. "He looked *into* the report" is much stronger than "He looked *at* the report." In another combination, "consist *in*" refers to inherent qualities, as in "The value of education consists *in* its enlarging the ability to comprehend cultures different from our own." *Consist of* is used to refer to component parts of an entity, as in "A government consists *of* the legislative, judicial, and executive branches."

P6 **up, down** *Up* sometimes carries the meaning of completion, as in *fill up, hurry up, drink up* (but "drink it *down*"). In the cases of *burn down* and *burn up, down* and *up* are intensives, and either phrase means total destruction by fire, either by being leveled to the ground or by going up in smoke. *Burn down* is used only with structures, or perhaps with candles, but *burn up* can refer to anything, such as important papers, etc. One would never use an intensive in burning rubbish or other trivial things. There are also differences between *close up* and *close down*. Whereas one might innocuously *close up* the house for the night, to *close down* a gambling casino suggests that force is used. The phrases *load up* and *load down*, which have the same basic meaning, are used in American English in an unusual way. *Load up* is used in the active, as in "*Load up* on food before we go camping." *Load down* is used in the passive, as in "She was *loaded down* with cans of food."

Conjugations and Principal Parts

(1) Conjugation of the Verb To Be

Infinitive: to be, be
Perfect Infinitive: to have been
Present Participle: being
Present Perfect Participle: having been
Past Participle: been

INDICATIVE MOOD

Person	*Singular*	*Plural*
	PRESENT TENSE	
First	I am	we are
Second	you are	you are
Third	he (she, it) is	they are
	FUTURE TENSE	
First	I shall be	we shall be
Second	you will be	you will be
Third	he (she, it) will be	they will be
	PAST TENSE	
First	I was	we were
Second	you were	you were
Third	he (she, it) was	they were

PRESENT PERFECT TENSE

First	I have been	we have been
Second	you have been	you have been
Third	he (she, it) has been	they have been

PAST PERFECT TENSE

First	I had been	we had been
Second	you had been	you had been
Third	he (she, it) will have been	they had been

FUTURE PERFECT TENSE

First	I shall have been	we shall have been
Second	you will have been	you will have been
Third	he (she, it) will have been	they will have been

IMPERATIVE MOOD

be

SUBJUNCTIVE MOOD

Present Tense: if I (you, he, she, it, we, they) be
Past Tense: if I (you, he, she, it, we, they) were

Conjugation of the Verb To Drive

ACTIVE VOICE   PASSIVE VOICE

Infinitive: to drive, drive   to be driven, be driven
Perfect Infinitive: to have driven   to have been driven
Present Participle: driving   being driven
Perfect Participle: having driven   having been driven
Past Participle: driven   been driven

INDICATIVE MOOD

Singular	*Plural*	*Singular*	*Plural*
		PRESENT TENSE	
1. I drive	we drive	I am driven	we are driven

2. you drive   you drive   you are driven   you are driven
3. he (she, it) drives   they drive   he (she, it) is driven   they are driven

FUTURE TENSE

1. I shall drive   we shall drive   I shall be driven   we shall be driven
2. you will drive   you will drive   you will be driven   you will be driven
3. he will drive   they will drive   he will be driven   they will be driven

PAST TENSE

1. I drove   we drove   I was driven   we were driven
2. you drove   you drove   you were driven   you were driven
3. he drove   they drove   he was driven   they were driven

PRESENT PERFECT TENSE

1. I have driven   we have driven   I have been driven   we have been driven
2. you have driven   you have driven   you have been driven   you have been driven
3. he has driven   they have driven   he has been driven   they have been driven

PAST PERFECT TENSE

1. I had driven   we had driven   I had been driven   we had been driven
2. you had driven   you had driven   you had been driven   you had been driven
3. he had driven   they had driven   he had been driven   they had been driven

FUTURE PERFECT TENSE

1. I shall have driven   we shall have driven   I shall have been driven   we shall have been driven
2. you will have driven   you will have driven   you will have been driven   you will have been driven
3. he will have driven   they will have driven   he will have been driven   they will have been driven

IMPERATIVE MOOD

drive

SUBJUNCTIVE MOOD

PRESENT TENSE

if I (you, he, she, it, we, they) drive

if I (you, he, she, it, we, they) be driven

PAST TENSE

if I (you, he, she, it, we, they) drove

if I (you, he, she, it, we, they) were driven

Principal Parts of Irregular Verbs

Regular verbs form the past tense and past participle by adding -ed (discover—discovered, cry—cried) or -d (raise—raised, tie—tied) to the infinitive. Verbs which do not follow these principles are known as irregular verbs. The following is a list of the principal parts of the most frequently used irregular verbs.

INFINITIVE AND PRESENT TENSE	PAST TENSE	PAST PARTICIPLE
arise	arose	arisen
awake	awoke, awaked	awaked, awoke
bear	bore	borne (born—passive voice)
beat	beat	beaten, beat
begin	began	begun
bend	bent	bent
bid (offer)	bid	bid
bid (command)	bade	bidden
bind	bound	bound
bite	bit	bitten, bit
blow	blew	blown
break	broke	broken
bring	brought	brought
broadcast	broadcast, broadcasted	broadcast, broadcasted

build	built	built
burst	burst	burst
buy	bought	bought
cast	cast	cast
catch	caught	caught
choose	chose	chosen
cling	clung	clung

INFINITIVE AND PRESENT TENSE	PAST TENSE	PAST PARTICIPLE
come	came	come
creep	crept	crept
deal	dealt	dealt
dive	dived, dove	dived
do	did	done
draw	drew	drawn
drink	drank	drunk
drive	drove	driven
eat	ate	eaten
fall	fell	fallen
feed	fed	fed
feel	felt	felt
fight	fought	fought
find	found	found
flee	fled	fled
fling	flung	flung
fly	flew	flown
forbear	forbore	forborne
forbid	forbade, forbad	forbidden
forget	forgot	forgotten, forgot
forgive	forgave	forgiven
forsake	forsook	forsaken
freeze	froze	frozen
get	got	got, gotten
give	gave	given
go	went	gone
grow	grew	grown
hang	hung (hanged—executed)	hung (hanged—executed
have (has)	had	had
hit	hit	hit
hold	held	held
hurt	hurt	hurt
kneel	knelt, kneeled	knelt
know	knew	known

lead	led	led
leap	leaped, leapt	leaped, leapt
leave	left	left
lend	lent	lent
let	let	let
lie	lay	lain
lose	lost	lost
make	made	made

INFINITIVE AND PRESENT TENSE	PAST TENSE	PAST PARTICIPLE
meet	met	met
put˙	put	put
read	read	read
rend	rent	rent
ride	rode	ridden
ring	rang	rung
rise	rose	risen
run	ran	run
see	saw	seen
seek	sought	sought
sell	sold	sold
send	sent	sent
set	set	set
shine	shone	shone
shrink	shrank, shrunk	shrunk, shrunken
sing	sang	sung
sink	sank	sunk
slay	slew	slain
sit	sat	sat
sleep	slept	slept
slide	slid	slid
sling	slung	slung
slink	slunk	slunk
speak	spoke	spoken
spring	sprang, sprung	sprung
steal	stole	stolen
stick	stuck	stuck
sting	stung	stung
stride	strode	strode, stridden
strike	struck	struck
swear	swore	sworn
sweat	sweat, sweated	sweated
sweep	swept	swept
swim	swam	swum

swing	swung	swung
take	took	taken
teach	taught	taught
tear	tore	torn
tell	told	told
think	thought	thought
thrive	throve, thrived	thrived, thriven
throw	threw	thrown
wake	waked, woke	waked, woken

INFINITIVE AND PRESENT TENSE	PAST TENSE	PAST PARTICIPLE
wear	wore	worn
weep	wept	wept
win	won	won
wind	wound	wound
work	worked, wrought	worked, wrought
wring	wrung	wrung
write	wrote	written

INDEX

faulty reference because of, 77-79
of pronoun and antecedent,
    70-75
of subject and verb, 61-70
Ain't, 69
Almost, position of, 91
Alright for *all right,* 208
Alumnus, alumna, alumni, alum-
    nae, 208
Among, between, 208
Amount, number, 208-209
An, a, 25, 207
Analogy in paragraph development,
    144-145
Anecdotes, use of, 183
Antecedents of pronouns, 6
    agreement error in reference, 77-79
    ambiguous reference, 75-76
    anticipatory reference, 74-75
    control of pronoun
        reference, 70
    definition of, 6
    implied reference, 74-75
    of demonstrative pronouns, 8-9
    undue separation of reference,
        76-77
Apostrophe, 132-133
    possessive form with gerunds,
        12-13
    to form plurals of letters, figures,
        etc., 132-133
    to form possessives, 4-5
    to indicate omissions, 132
Appearance of manuscript, 193-194
Appositives, 53
    case forms of, 10, 79, 81
    function of, 53
Appropriateness, 115-116, 188-190
Apt, likely, liable, 209
Aren't I?, 69
Arrangement of words for emphasis,
    105-108
Article, 25
As, like, 209
Assert, claim, 209
Averse, adverse, 207
Avert, advert, 208
Avoidance
    of abbreviations, 199
    of generalizations, 189

of immodesty, 189
of inaccuracy, 188
of intemperateness, 189
of irony, 189
of monotony, 116-118
of sarcasm, 189
of scorn, 189

Balance for emphasis, 111-113
Beginning a paper, 181-186
Beside, besides, 209
Between, among, 209
Brackets, 133
Bring, take, 209

Can, may, 209
Capitals
    first word of sentences, 59
    in footnotes, 195
    in quotations, 134-135
    proper nouns, 2-3
Case
    declension of personal pronouns, 7
    declension of relative pronouns, 7-8
    definition of, 9
    nominative of pronouns, 7, 10-11
    objective of pronouns, 7, 11-12
    possessive of nouns, 4-5, 9
    possessive of pronouns, 7, 12-13
Case usage
    after *to be,* 10-11, 80-81
    for appositives, 10, 79, 81
    for coordinate noun and pronoun,
        10, 82
    for determiners, 12-13
    for non-animate things, 4-5
    for nouns in a series, 4
    for object of verb or preposition,
        11-12, 79, 81
    for object of verbal, 11-12, 81
    for predicate noun or pronoun,
        11-12, 80
    for subject of infinitive, 11-12, 16
    for subject of verb, 10, 79, 80
    for two nouns referring to the same
        person, 4
Cause and effect, use of, in paragraph
    development, 146

226